BRUCE & STAN'S

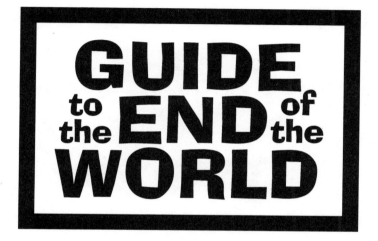

GUIDE to the END of the WORLD

BRUCE BICKEL and STAN JANTZ

HARVEST HOUSE PUBLISHERS
Eugene, Oregon 97402

Cover design by Left Coast Design, Portland, Oregon

Interior design by Ty Pauls, Harvest House Publishers

Prophecy charts based on those in *Fast Facts On Bible Prophecy* by Thomas Ice and Timothy Demy (Harvest House Publishers, 1997)

BRUCE & STAN'S GUIDE TO THE END OF THE WORLD

Copyright © 1999 by Bruce Bickel and Stan Jantz
Published by Harvest House Publishers
Eugene, Oregon 97402

ISBN: 0-7394-0464-4

Contents

About the Authors

Bruce Bickel spent three weeks as an aspiring actor before spending 20 years as a perspiring attorney. His flare for theatrics goes to waste in his law practice (he specializes in estate planning and probate). He is a gifted communicator, and his speeches, seminars, and sermons serve as the outlet for all his backed-up comedic and dramatic talents. His presentations of the gospel message are filled with truth, clarity, and passion (and a lot of flailing arm motions). Residing in Fresno, California, the Bickel family consists of Bruce, his wife, Cheryl, and their children, Lindsey and Matt. Bruce and Cheryl serve as co-chairs of the Parents Council, and Bruce is on the Board of Trustees at Westmont College, where Lindsey attends.

Stan Jantz is the Public Relations Manager for Berean Christian Stores. Christian retailing is a family tradition in Stan's family. His father owned a chain of Christian bookstores for 45 years, and Stan has been directly involved in the industry for 25 years. Because he has literally grown up around Christian books and Bibles ("I was raised by a set of Bible commentaries," he says), Stan brings a unique perspective to his collaborative writing ("First rule," he advises, "never use the word *collaborative* in a sentence"). Stan lives in Fresno with his wife, Karin, and their two children, Hillary and Scott. In addition to their involvement in a local church, Stan and Karin serve as co-chairs of the Parents Council at Biola University, where Hillary attends.

Bruce and Stan have collaborated (there's that word again) on eight books, with combined sales of more than a half million copies (unfortunately it's only the *first* half). *Bruce & Stan's Guide to God* was the first and *Bruce & Stan's Guide to the Bible* is the second in a series (they hope a *long* series) of "user-friendly" books Bruce and Stan are writing. Their passion is to present biblical truth in a clear, consise, and correct manner that encourages people to connect with the living God in a meaningful way (which rules out finding God by contemplating your navel).

A Note from the Authors

You may be curious about how the world is going to end—about the future of the planet and of the human race, about what is going to happen when you die, and that sort of thing. So are we. We are *curious,* but we're not *worried.* You see, even though we don't know all of the specific details about *what* is going to happen or the exact dates of *when* things will occur, we know the overall plan and we have taken the necessary steps to prepare ourselves. We aren't worried about the final outcome.

But we are curious about what is going to happen and who will be involved. That's why we wrote this book on the end of the world.

If you have read our biographies, you probably noticed that we don't have any theological or scientific credentials. Does that disqualify us from writing a book about the end of the world? We don't think so. In fact, we think that we are the perfect guys to write this kind of book. The whole point of a book like this is that you don't have to be an astrophysicist, a seminary graduate, or a member of the Psychic Friends Network to understand how the world is going to end. All the information you need is readily available. You just need to know where to look, and we'll help you do that.

As we guide you through the adventure of learning about life and death and beyond, we won't get preachy. We'll just give it to you straight. And so that you know we've consulted the experts, we've listed the resources we used at the end of every chapter. We've also asked several Bible scholars to review this book for accuracy. We hope this gives you some assurance that we aren't a couple of wackos (although our families are not always convinced about that).

None of us will ever know in this lifetime all the mysteries of the future, but you can know enough to make the choices that will secure your destiny. Like the song says: you don't have to know what the future holds, if you know who holds the future.

Bruce Bickel

Stan Jantz

Fresno, California

Introduction

How do you react when you see some guy standing on the street corner with a sign that says: "The End of the World is Coming"? Do you snicker because you think he's a goofy eccentric? Or do you get a little worried that maybe he knows something you don't?

Let's face it. We all have different degrees of concern and curiosity about *if, how,* and *when* the world is going to end. Maybe you haven't really given it a thought. Maybe you can't think about anything else. May we suggest this quick quiz to determine your "End Times Tolerance":

You Are "End Times Impressionable" if . . .

- ✓ You don't shop at warehouse stores like Costco because you don't think you'll be around long enough to eat a 37-pound box of cornflakes.
- ✓ You are afraid to get money from the automated teller machine because the bank assigned you a PIN number of 666.
- ✓ After watching one of those global-disaster movies, you boldly proclaim: "That could never really happen," and then you quickly glance around to see if anyone is nodding in agreement.
- ✓ You freaked out when you went to church and found no one there (only to realize later that you showed up an hour early because you forgot to change the clock for daylight savings time).
- ✓ An earthquake has you scrambling to find that Bible you haven't read since eighth grade.

If we have just described you, then start reading chapter 1 right away, and don't stop until you can pop your head out from under the covers. You must be scared spitless, so you need to get a grip on what is actually going to happen and how you can deal with it.

Now let's test for the other end of the spectrum:

You Are "End Times Insensitive" if . . .

✓ You think the "Apocalypse" is a car manufactured by Toyota.

✓ All of the talk about the "Doomsday Event" has you baffled. You can't figure out why everyone is making such a fuss about a WWF wrestling match.

✓ You ignore people when they fret about the political turmoil in the Middle East because you don't vote in New York.

✓ The increasing frequency of floods, earthquakes, droughts, and other environmental disasters is of no concern to you (except for ruining the coffee bean harvests and raising the cost of a Starbuck's latte).

✓ You're skeptical about a cataclysmic end of the world since it didn't already happen during a John Tesh concert.

If these statements describe you, then you need to get a clue. What rock have you been hiding under? Or did you just return from a decade-long vacation in Antarctica without the luxury of CNN or *USA Today*? Can't you decipher the proverbial "handwriting on the wall"? The odds-makers are taking bets on when this global popsicle stand is going to blow. You'd better read this book to help get up to speed with what's going on . . . and hurry.

What You'll Find Inside

A lot of books have been written about the end of the world, and we have read many of them. Unfortunately, most of them are so hypertechnical and confusing that they make you wish for a swift end of the world just to stop the throbbing in your head. And they are filled with phraseology like "dispensational premillenialism eschatology" (which sounds to us like some sort of bowel disease). We'll buck that trend by providing you with a book in which we try to:

✓ *Focus on the big picture.* We'll give you an overview. Oh, sure, along the way we'll stop to mention a few highlights of particular interest, but we won't get bogged down in the details that you don't really care about. When we're done, you'll have a good orientation.

✓ *Stay objective.* We won't take some minority viewpoint or off-the-wall interpretation and try to cram it into your cranium. (We are opposed to all forms of cranium cramming.) Instead, we'll give you the facts and clearly distinguish between assumptions and speculation. On issues where there are legitimate opposing theories, we'll present the different perspectives.

✓ *Make it personal.* We think we know what questions are on your mind—they're the same ones on ours. So we'll anticipate, ask, and answer your personal questions like:

- If the world ends during your lifetime, are you going to suffer?

- What happens when you die?

- Are you going to get judged and punished for everything bad you have ever done (and is everyone else going to find out)?

- Is hell a real place (and how do you avoid it)?

- Does heaven exist (and how do you make your reservation)?

These are certainly heartfelt, legitimate questions, and you deserve direct answers.

✓ *Keep it simple.* We have been trying for years to impress our families, and it hasn't worked, so we won't start on you. No effort will be made to dazzle you with the breadth of our knowledge or the depth of our understanding. Just take our word for it. (Stan is deep, and Bruce is wide.)

✓ *Be relevant.* We know what you're thinking: If it doesn't affect you, then it doesn't really matter. We agree, but we're convinced that this whole end-of-the-world thing *does* affect you. One way or the other, sooner or later, it is going to come to an end for you. We'll let you know what you can do *now* to be prepared for *then*.

Why You Need to Read This Book

Everybody has a theory about how the world is going to end. Religious scholars look to ancient sacred manuscripts and predict the coming judgment of God. Environmentalists point to the dangers of global warming and environmental calamities. Scientists warn of meteor showers which will pummel the earth. And the publishers of the supermarket tabloids predict an invasion of mutant alien creatures who are descendants of Elvis. Whom can you believe? What information is trustworthy and reliable?

It is our opinion (and we don't think that we are going out on a limb here) that the Bible is the only reliable source for information about the end of the world. But you won't have to take our opinion for it. We'll show you why the Bible can be trusted. Then you can decide for yourself.

Knowing what is going to happen when you die may change the way you live. The Bible says that God has this intricate plan all worked out, and everything is going according to schedule. He is going ahead with it whether you believe it or not. He won't cancel the whole thing just because you deny it. So we think you owe it to yourself to see what the Bible says about God's plan for the world—and for you. Your life will depend on it...and your life after death will be determined by it.

This Book Is for You If . . .

✓ You are intrigued by those movies which show the world poised for disaster. Now it's time to move from fiction to reality (because you have a sneaking suspicion that Stallone, Schwarzenegger and Willis will be useless when it really counts).

✓ All the talk about the new millennium has got you curious about the future of planet Earth. You don't know if the Bible has all the answers, but it seems like a good place to start.

✓ You have some familiarity with the Bible. You have heard of Moses, King David, and the baby Jesus. Those stories are nice, but they are ancient history. You want to know what the Bible says is in store for *you*.

✓ You were channel surfing and ran across a religious program featuring a prominent televangelist. He was all red in the face and the veins on the side of his head were pulsating as he ranted and raved about fire and brimstone. Frankly, you question whether God would really send people to hell after they die. It doesn't seem to be a very "loving" thing to do. But just in case your hunch is wrong, you want to get a little more information.

✓ All this end-of-the-world stuff scares you a little bit. (Actually, it scares you a lot, so you try not to think about it.) But your mind is spinning with questions, and you don't know who to ask. Your friends don't know any more than you do, and you are embarrassed to ask anyone else. Although you've tried to find some help in the Bible, it didn't help that much because you didn't know how to get started, and the symbolism didn't make any sense at all. You are more confused now than you were before.

✓ You are a longtime churchgoer. The "end times" subject fascinates you. You sat through a few Sunday school classes on the subject, and a Bible study or two on the books of Daniel and Revelation. But you spent all of the time looking at the trees and never saw what the forest looked like. You are frustrated because it seems like you can never figure out how all this stuff fits together.

✓ You are a skeptic and proud of it. Religious people have been predicting for years that the world was coming to an end soon. Well, it didn't. They are now dead and you're not. You aren't going to be swayed by what other people say; you want to investigate the Bible predictions for yourself.

How to Use This Book

The Bible describes the end of the world with prophecies and symbolism that can be tedious and confusing. We don't want our book to add to your bewilderment, so we have designed it to be reader-friendly. After all, when it comes to reading about how your life is going to end, you don't want to doze off and miss something. To get maximum use of this book, watch for these features:

1. Icons. If you are a scanner more than a reader, we have loaded the margins with icons to let you know what is happening in the text. Here is what each icon means:

Big Idea. Don't miss this discussion. It is a major point.

Key Verse. All throughout the book we will quote Bible verses so you can easily see for yourself what the Bible says. Now, we wouldn't want to say that some verses are important and others are not. So let's agree that this icon marks the ones that are more essential to the topic at hand than the others.

Glad You Asked. Remember that we promised to keep the discussion relevant and personal to you by anticipating, asking, and answering your questions. Well, this icon marks the places where we do that.

It's a Mystery. One of the reasons we aren't intimidated by writing this book is because we don't pretend to have all of the answers. (No one does.) And we aren't afraid to admit it. This icon marks a discussion which presents an issue or question for which the answer is known only by God.

Learn the Lingo. The subject of the "end times" has a language all of its own. We try to stay away from the really technical jargon as often as possible. But there are certain terms which you'll need to know. Whenever we use this icon, you'll find important terminology for which we will give a clear definition in "plain English."

Bruce Says . . . Stan Says. From time to time, we just can't help interrupting ourselves with a personal story or our own point of view. Humor us, okay?

Jump to. Many times we will refer to a concept that is discussed at length elsewhere in the book. In case you are interested in reading ahead on a subject or covering something you skipped, this icon will tell you where to look.

Dig Deeper. This icon indicates one of the most important parts of this book. At the end of each chapter we will provide you with the titles and authors of some of our favorite books and resources just in case you want to do more in-depth reading on the subject of that chapter.

2. Think About It. Starting at page 329, we have listed several questions for each chapter. We think you will find these questions helpful, whether you are studying the book alone or in a group. These aren't questions which can be answered with a simple "yes" or "no" answer. A little head-scratching may be required. But don't worry about getting a wrong answer. Most of the questions ask for your personal response, so whatever answer you give can be correct.

3. Index. We won't be offended if you want to skip around in the book and just look up the topics of greatest interest to you. You can use the index to help you find what you are looking for.

We Love It When People Talk Back

We would like to hear from you after you have read the book. Give us your comments and questions. (Compliments are welcomed, and criticisms are accepted.) The easiest way to contact us is by e-mail at:

guide@bruceandstan.com

which you can send directly or access through our web site at:

www.bruceandstan.com

Our web site lists information about the other books in our "Bruce & Stan's Guide to..." series, as well as our other books and meaningless Bruce & Stan trivia. Or if you are clinging to a sentimental attachment with the postal service, you can send your cards, letters, and parcels to:

Bruce and Stan
P.O. Box 25565
Fresno, CA 93729-5565

One More Comment Before You Get Started

The stuff you are about to encounter can be pretty scary. We will be talking about wars, disasters, and worldwide calamity. Even worse than that is the reality that there will be eternal pain and torment for many people. But there is good news, too. And we're excited that you are going to learn about all the great and wonderful things that God has planned for you at the end of the world. In the pages which follow, you can find answers for living life on earth and beyond.

> *But we are looking forward to the new heavens and new earth he has promised, a world where everyone is right with God. And so, dear friends, while you are waiting for these things to happen, make every effort to live a pure and blameless life. And be at peace with God* (2 Peter 3:13-15).

PART I:

WHAT IN THE WORLD IS GOING ON?

We who live in this nervous age would be wise to meditate on our lives and our days long and often before the face of God and on the edge of eternity. For we are made for eternity as certainly as we are made for time, and as responsible moral beings we must deal with both.

—*A. W. Tozer*

There are two great questions in life. The first one is, "Where did I come from?" The second is, "What happens when I die?" It's the second question that we're going to deal with in this chapter. In fact, this whole book is about that question. We cannot help but be interested in the end of the world as it is a topic which affects us all.

In this chapter we're going to consider the various ways you can look at your life and the end of the world. To do that we're going to help you identify your personal *worldview*. Then we'll try to answer that all-important question: "Are we really in the end times?" Later in Part I we'll give you some ideas as to where you can look for answers to the basic questions about your life and the end of the world. So if you're ready, let's begin. Let's try to figure out where this world and your life are headed.

Bruce & Stan

Chapter 1

The End Is
Near . . . or Is It?

*O*nce upon a time there was a life. Your life. Your life had a beginning—you were born on a certain date, which you celebrate once a year—and you grew up, or at least you're in the process of growing up (some people wonder if Bruce and Stan have grown up yet—we're not sure).

Think about your life for a moment. Reflect. Ponder. Mentally run through the highs and lows. Bring yourself up to date, to this very moment. Are you happy with your life so far? Sure, there is always room for improvement, but overall, you're doing okay, right?

Now set your own life aside for a moment and think of the world around you. Picture the big blue marble we call Earth sitting in space, the only planet in the universe capable of sustaining life (including yours). Like you, this world had a beginning and it has had a life (we call it history).

It's Time to Think About the End

As long as we can agree that both your life and the world had a beginning, then we can move to the most important issue you will ever deal with. It's also the subject of this book. Are you ready? Here goes:

Just as your life had a beginning, your life will have an end.

Wow, is that ever profound! But there's more:

Just as the world had a beginning, the world will have an end.

Bet you never expected to encounter such deep thinking in this book. Well, we're deceptively deep. And so are you. And it's time to start thinking about your life and the world and how they're both going to end. We're not trying to be morbid here, and our intention is not to encourage you to become preoccupied with death (there's enough of that going on already). We want you to think *beyond* death. We want you to think beyond the *end* of life as we know it by asking yourself two very important questions:

✓ What happens when I die?

✓ What happens when this old world finally comes to an end?

People Want to Know What's Out There

It seems like the whole world wants to know what the future holds. Just look at the fascination with the millennium. Is there something magical about the world having another thousand-year birthday, or is it all a bunch of hype (be patient, we'll get to that)? And then there are all those psychic hot lines. People are paying good money to hear personal "advice" from cable hucksters who look like they belong in a carnival sideshow guessing your weight.

Hollywood isn't immune to "future fever" either. Some of the most ambitious recent movies have focused on "conspiracy" or "end times" scenarios. Whether it's a bunch of alien invaders or a natural space disaster, the world stands on the brink of extinction until two FBI agents or a tough guy with a perpetual three-day beard save it for another day (or at least another movie).

Then there are those bestselling books about the afterlife, like the one in which some guy claims to talk to the dead. At first we thought the whole thing was a joke, but when we saw how intelligent-looking people were pleading with the psychic to contact their dead friends and relatives, we realized that many people are very serious about wanting to know what lies beyond the grave.

What's Your Worldview?

What you think about the future depends a lot on your *worldview*. In *Bruce & Stan's Guide to God*, we said that all of us have a worldview, or personal belief system. Our worldview colors everything we do in one way or another. It determines how we behave, the choices we make, and often how we feel. Dr. Paul Cox, a professor at Biola University, says that a worldview "gives an overall framework to one's life, thus giving direction and purpose—whether good or bad."

When it comes to the future, there are really three basic worldviews. In each one, notice how the perspective of how things are going to *end* is related to the view of how things *began*.

1. Everything will stay the same. There was a time when some scientists believed in the "steady state model" of the universe. They claimed that the universe never had a beginning and has always existed in a steady state. It has always pretty much been the same as it is now. You probably won't find many people who buy into this theory today. Science almost universally believes that the universe had a beginning, that it has been expanding, and that someday it will collapse and end. So much for the steady state.

About the only worldview you can get out of this notion that everything stays the same is *monism*, which believes that God is in everything, and everything is God. *Pantheism*, which believes in multiple gods (Hinduism is the best example), is a cousin of monism. In this worldview, history is nothing more than a series of cycles. People get reincarnated as flies (if they haven't lived a good life) or more important beings like cows and Shirley MacLaine (if they've lived a good life). So in this model your life and the world don't actually have an end. You simply exist in an endless loop.

2. Everything will get better. The idea that our world and the people in it are progressing to a better place is ultimately based on a *naturalistic* worldview. This is probably the trendiest worldview in the world today. It is also the worldview that leaves God out of the picture completely. Here's how it works.

✓ The *material* or *natural* world is all there is.

✓ The universe had a beginning, but it was an *impersonal* beginning.

✓ From that impersonal beginning, life has evolved from simple single-cell beings into complex beings, the ultimate example of which are human beings.

✓ God is nowhere to be found in this worldview (atheism is a cousin). Rather, man is the measure of all things.

✓ As people improve, the world will get better.

This belief in the improvability of human beings is often referred to as *humanism.* It is a philosophy which thrives under the naturalistic worldview. To the humanist, the future is bright, hopeful, and wonderful. Forget all those pesky wars and the senseless violence. Forget diseases with no cure and natural disasters unlike anything seen in world history. We are getting better, and so is our world.

TECHNOLOGY AND THE HUMANIST

Technology is one of the keys to humanistic optimism, as it frees us to improve ourselves on a personal level. We're not just talking about microwaves, cell phones, and ever-improving toasters. Some humanists talk openly about the day when biogenetics and DNA research will enable us to improve the quality of the human race. But didn't Hitler already try that with his technological marvel, the gas chamber? Others simply want their computer to give them more time.

Ironically, even though a personal God doesn't exist in this worldview, one of its goals is personal spiritual growth. However, it's the human spirit that matters. And it's our choices that count. Because we are the center of the universe, we will determine its fate. David Noebel suggests in *Understanding the Times* that the humanist ultimately sees his philosophy as the only hope for mankind. "Neither God, nor the environment, nor any man adhering to any worldview other than Humanism, can lead our world into the future."

Of course, there's that pesky scientific theory that says the universe is going to collapse someday. No problem, say the humanists. By the time it does, we will have figured out a way to save ourselves. Who knows, we may even be rescued by aliens; otherwise, we'll just find another universe to inhabit.

3. Everything will get worse. The third view of the future holds that life as we know it is in a constant state of degradation. Whether it's your desk, your body, or the universe, everything naturally moves from order to disorder, and from more energy to less energy. Put more simply, everything that lives slowly dies. Therefore, the world is not getting better. It's getting worse, and it will continue to get worse.

The *Christian* worldview embraces this viewpoint, but with a more personal application. Here's how it works:

- ✓ A personal, eternal, self-existent God brought all things into existence.
- ✓ God created the heavens and the earth and human beings in a perfect state.
- ✓ God's human creatures rebelled against Him, bringing sin and death to humankind and the world.
- ✓ Even though the world and its inhabitants are in a sinful state, God is still in control.
- ✓ Under God's control, the universe is orderly and operates according to physical laws.
- ✓ Under God's control, the universe is an open system, which means, according to Dr. Cox, "God can intervene and man can interrupt. Man can pollute his environment and affect his future. Such action is a possibility because the system is orderly and open."

✓ God intervened in human history when He sent Jesus Christ, who brought hope to a fallen humanity.

✓ God is in the process of bringing history to a fitting conclusion, which will happen when Jesus returns to earth a second time.

Don't get us wrong. We are not suggesting that you become obsessed with the future and the end of the world. We are well aware of the weird and wacky positions people have taken about the end of the world through the centuries—often in the name of God. Who can forget the haunting images of

---

Bruce and Stan's
"End-of-the-World Evaluation"

Do you agree that everyone has a worldview? Did we list yours? If not, describe your worldview here, and be sure to include your own end-of-the-world scenario.

_____

_____

_____

_____

_____

_____

Marshall Applewhite's Heaven's Gate cult, whose members ate poisoned pudding so they could leave this dying world and join the alien ship which was lurking behind the Hale-Bopp comet?

It's entirely possible to get a prophecy fixation. We don't want you to go there. In fact, if you're reading this book hoping for a new "theory" on how the world is going to end, you will probably be disappointed. However, if you want to know God's plan for the ages—and His plan for you—so that your life will be more meaningful now, then you've come to the right place.

How to Have a Healthy View of the Future

There's a difference between having a healthy view of the future and worrying about it. For one thing, the future is relative. It can be as *near* as tomorrow or as *distant* as the end of your life.

Jesus was very clear about the *near* future when He said:

So don't worry about having enough food or drink or clothing. Why be like the pagans who are so deeply concerned about these things? (Matthew 6:31,32).

Worrying about how you are going to live tomorrow can drain your energy and minimize your effectiveness today. Jesus was very clear that we are to seek the things of God first.

CRAZED FUTURISTS
WE HAVE KNOWN

Besides the Heaven's Gate group, there have been in the past and continue to be many weird and wacky ideas about the end of the world. For example:

✓ In the 1970s, cult leader Jim Jones led hundreds of people from his California church, known as the People's Temple, to Guyana in South America. They established a settlement known as Jonestown to wait for the end of the world. In 1978 Jones ordered the members of his cult to commit suicide because "it was time." More than 900 people died.

✓ In Russia a self-appointed messiah named Vissarion has attracted 5000 followers to his City of the Sun in Siberia. He speaks of "the coming end" and has told his followers that suicide is not a sin. Our feeling on this one is that people who volunteer to go to Siberia to follow a guy who is enamored with suicide probably don't value their lives very much.

✓ A group of nearly 200 people moved from Taiwan to Garland, Texas (they claimed it was God's land . . . Gar-land . . . God's land . . . get it?), to wait for God, who was supposed to return to earth (to Garland, of course) in a flying saucer on March 31, 1998. Heng-ming Chen, the leader of "God Saves the Earth Flying Saucer Association," claims to talk to God through his hand. He has also offered to surrender his life to his followers if his prophecies turn up false (he's not big on suicide). At last report no one knew where Chen was, and most of the members, who had purchased round-trip plane tickets, were on their way back home.

Cult expert and theologian Douglas Groothuis says that we'll be seeing more and more of these strange and some-times dangerous groups pop up, especially on the Internet. "I think that the online context can remove people from a proper understanding of reality and the proper tests for truth," he says.

But what about the *distant* future? How concerned are we to be about things to come, especially things occurring at the end of the world? The followers of Jesus asked Him that very question 2000 years ago. "When will all this take place? And will there be any sign ahead of time to signal your return and the end of the world?" (Matthew 24:3).

Jesus was very specific in His answer. He gave all kinds of clues about *how* the world would end (we'll talk about these in future chapters). And He said something very interesting about *when* the end would come:

No one knows the day or the hour when these things will happen, not even the angels in heaven or the Son himself. Only the Father knows (Matthew 24:36).

So what are we to do? How are we to live in light of this uncertainty? Again, Jesus gives us an answer:

You must be ready all the time. For the Son of Man will come when least expected (Matthew 24:44).

Be Ready, Wise, and Watchful

A healthy view of the future means that we are to be *ready, wise,* and *watchful.*

 ## Why Dating the Future Doesn't Work

It's not just the cults that get involved in end-times hysteria or date setting. Many Christians throughout history were convinced that Jesus would return in their lifetime. Historian Richard Kyle has written about hundreds of "Millennial Groups" throughout history who taught that the end of the world was at hand. Here is just a sampling:

✓ The first-century Christians were convinced that Jesus was going to return in their lifetime. Hippolytus, a Roman priest and theologian, predicted that Christ would return in A.D. 500.

✓ Millennium fever swept the world 1000 years ago as many clergy feared the rise of the Antichrist. Many believers were convinced that Jesus was coming back at that time.

✓ The Shakers, who came to America from England in

Be ready. You never know what's going to happen to the world. All it takes is a bomb and one guy like Saddam on a bad day and—*voilà*— World War III. And even if some lunatic doesn't push the Big Button, you need to be ready on a personal level. You never know when you're going to step off the curb and be run over by the proverbial beer truck. As the Bible says,

---

1774, were a "millennial church." That is, they believed the millennium was at hand. The Shakers were "fanatically anti-sex" (no wonder they built such great furniture). They couldn't even marry. Theoretically, if their ideas prevailed, the human race would end. That was okay with the Shakers. Since the end of the world was at hand anyway, there was no reason for the human race to procreate.

✓ The date setting seems to have intensified in this century. Forty million copies of Hal Lindsey's book *The Late Great Planet Earth* have been sold since 1970. Lindsey has never really set a date for the end of the world, but he has strongly suggested that it will happen in our lifetime, which he calls "The Terminal Generation."

✓ In 1988 hundreds of thousands of people bought a booklet entitled *88 Reasons Why Jesus Will Return in 1988*. The book went out of print on January 1, 1989, and the author hasn't been seen or heard from since.

How do you know what will happen tomorrow? For your life is like the morning fog—it's here a little while, then it's gone (James 4:14).

Be wise. Don't fear tomorrow, but be very clear about what God has planned for the future. In this book, we are going to do our best to give you a clear picture of God's plan for the future. There are many mysteries about the future, and we'll be honest and tell you when we don't know. But we will point you to those places where the Bible is clear about what to expect, so that nothing that happens should surprise you. The more you know about which way this world is going tomorrow, the better you can live your life today:

So be careful how you live, not as fools but as those who are wise. Make the most of every opportunity for doing good in these evil days. Don't act thoughtlessly, but try to understand what the Lord wants you to do (Ephesians 5:15-17).

Be watchful. Keeping watch over something means guarding it against intruders. This applies to your house and your heart. Just as you wouldn't want a thief to sneak into your house when you're physically asleep, you don't want the world to end when you're spiritually asleep. Jesus was very specific on this subject:

Watch out! Don't let me find you living in careless ease and drunkenness, and filled with the worries of this life. Don't let that day catch you unaware, as in a trap. For that day will come upon everyone living on the earth. Keep a constant watch. And pray that, if possible, you may escape these horrors and stand before the Son of Man (Luke 21:34-36).

Are We Really in the End Times?

Before we go any further, specifically dealing with "the end of the world" (also known as the *end times*), it's only fair to give you our answer to the question everyone is asking:

Are we really in the end times?

We're going to get a little cute on you here (how can we be any other way?) and tell you, "We don't know, but . . . " We're not trying to duck the question. We really do want to give you a straight answer. Here it is:

The end of the world will occur in your lifetime.

Now the "cute" part is that we can make this statement and know that we are 100 percent right. The Bible says that the world is going to end, but that no one knows "the day or the hour." So it's possible that Jesus will return to earth—setting off the events leading to the end of the world—at any time, including your lifetime and ours.

Bruce & Stan's
"End Times: Are We There Yet?" Test

The Bible predicts events and circumstances which will be "signs" that the world (as we know it) is coming to an end. We'll get to all of the specifics in chapters 6 and 7. For now, just take this little test by answering "yes" or "no" to whether you have seen any of these "signs of the times."

_____ **An increase in earthquakes**
Hint: Ask any Californian.

_____ **An increase in unpredictable weather patterns**
Hint: Remember the recent visit from El Niño.

_____ **Pollution of our planet**
Hint: Ask Al Gore or the Sierra Club.

_____ **Cataclysmic events in the sky**
Hint: Remember the Hale-Bopp comet.

_____ **Wars and rumors of wars**
Hint: Read any newspaper.

_____ **Territorial boundary disputes in the Middle East**
Hint: Keep reading the same newspaper.

_____ **Famines**
Hint: Think about Pakistan and India and some of the African nations, to name a few.

_____ **The formation of the nation of Israel**
Hint: From about A.D. 70 until 1948, the

nation of Israel did not exist. In 1948, Israel achieved its independent national status. Biblical scholars had been predicting this for centuries.

_____ **The gospel of Jesus Christ will be preached around the world**
Hint: Satellite broadcasts

_____ **Instant worldwide communication**
Hint: CNN and the Internet

_____ **An increase in knowledge**
Hint: Sociologists say that we are in "the information age."

_____ **Move toward a one-world government**
Hint: Passports from separate British and European countries have the name of the country on the cover, but at the top are the words "European Community."

_____ **Move toward a one-world economy**
Hint: Think about ATMs, the home-shopping network, and on-line shopping.

_____ **People claiming to be the Messiah**
Hint: Remember the Heaven's Gate cult.

_____ **An increase in the wickedness of the human race**
Hint: Watch the evening news.

_____ **An increase in immorality**
Hint: Keep watching the evening news.

_____ **An increase in materialism and self-centeredness**
Hint: Sociologists say we are living in the "me" generation.

Don't Wait Too Late

A lot of people will try to tell you that certain things have to happen before the world comes to an end. They'll say it's the new millennium, or certain world conditions, or some evil national leader. Don't be lulled into a false sense of security, thinking you have more time. There's no event or person who will trigger the end of the world, except for One: Jesus Christ. The end of the world will happen only when Jesus returns to earth, and that could happen any time. That is what we mean when we refer to the *imminent* return of Christ.

Here's the other part of our answer: Even if the end of the world doesn't occur during your lifetime, it will end when you die—at least for you. Many people believe that even after you die, you still have the chance to get things right with God. But the Bible is very clear about the next step after death:

It is destined that each person dies only once and after that comes judgment (Hebrews 9:27).

You see, when you die, the final curtain will come down. The world as you know it will end. And you will be immediately ushered into eternity to await judgment. It will be too late to change your mind. Only one thing will count: your relationship with God.

Bruce and Stan to the Rescue

Chapter 2

Actually, we're not the ones who will rescue you. We're more like messengers with a very important message, which is contained in the rest of this book. More importantly, the message is found in the Bible, which we'll talk about in chapter 2.

Meanwhile, before we end this chapter, we want to leave you with three things:

Our Reassurance

Yes, the world is going to end someday. Whether you're here to see it happen doesn't really matter. What matters is that there is a way to prepare yourself for the end, and it isn't eating poisoned pudding or building a bomb shelter. It also doesn't involve doing all kinds of stuff in this life so that you'll be included in the voyage to the next one. Our reassurance is that everybody—regardless of age, race, ability, or economic standing—can be prepared for the end of the world and live through it.

It doesn't matter what you've done or what you haven't done. If you're a member of the human race, you qualify to receive the invitation of a lifetime—the invitation to voluntarily join Club Forever. Membership is open to all, and more than likely you've already been invited. If you don't remember getting an invitation, or you've somehow misplaced it or can't remember what it says, here's a copy.

Our Invitation

To Whom It May Concern
(THAT'S YOU)

You are hereby invited to join Club Forever. Membership is free, and the benefits start immediately, although no one knows exactly when the Voyage to Eternity will begin. The Captain of the Voyage is away right now, but He will be returning at any time. Meanwhile, He has asked that you observe these rules of eternal safety as found in the Eternal Voyage Manual:

1. *Realize that the Captain cares about you. In fact, He loves you more than you'll ever know* (John 3:16).

2. *It is impossible for you to qualify for membership in Club Forever on your own* (Romans 3:23).

3. *Don't worry. Even though you don't qualify and can't afford the cost, the Captain has paid the price for you* (Romans 5:8).

4. *It's futile to look for another way to join Club Forever. This is the only way* (John 14:6).

5. *To accept this invitation, all you have to do is take the Captain's words to heart. Believe that what He said is true and then tell others about it* (Romans 10:9).

Our Promise

You don't have to wait until the end—when the Eternal Voyage begins—to enjoy the benefits of membership in Club Forever. There's an immediate benefit in knowing the truth about tomorrow. It's called *peace . . .* peace of mind . . . peace of heart. When you know where you're going when you die—when you know where you're going when the world comes to an end—your life will take on new meaning and you will be at peace with your future.

You will also fulfill your longing for eternity. You see, the reason there is so much interest in the end of the world and the world beyond and life after death is that God has put these ideas into each of us. Buried deep within the Bible in a book written by King Solomon, considered to be the wisest man who ever lived, are these immortal words:

God has made everything beautiful for its own time. He has planted eternity in the human heart, but even so, people cannot see the whole scope of God's work from beginning to end (Ecclesiastes 3:11).

When you invite the eternal God into your life by accepting Jesus Christ, the Captain of your salvation (Hebrews 2:10, KJV), you literally bring eternity into your heart. You have the distinct advantage of being able to see things from eternity's perspective.

> *T*he world of time is no longer the sole reality of which we are aware. A second Reality hovers, quickens, quivers, stirs, energizes us, breaks in upon us and in love embraces us, together with all things, within Himself. We live our lives at two levels simultaneously, the level of time and the level of the Timeless.
>
> —Thomas Kelly

Five Ways to Get a Smart Start on the End

Here are five ways to help you be smart about the end of the world:

1. Develop a balanced view of the end of the world. Don't become obsessed with it (you know, one of those people who wear only black and stay up late so they can listen to those all-night radio shows that mostly discuss UFOs). On the other hand, deal with the end of the world as a reality.

2. Make sure you are square with God, who has a plan in place for you and for the end of the world (more about that in chapter 2).

3. Begin reading the Bible systematically, which means on a regular basis and in an orderly fashion (more about that in chapter 3). Don't focus all your reading on the prophecy passages in the Bible. Remember that the Bible is a guide for all of life, not just the end of the world.

4. Read reliable books about God, the Bible, and the end of the world (we list some really good ones at the end of each chapter in the "Dig Deeper" section). Also, keep up with current events so you can relate to people who have questions about what's going on in the world.

5. Pray to God and ask Him to give you wisdom, understanding, and peace of mind as you think about these critical and sometimes disturbing issues.

"What's That Again?"

1. Just as your life had a beginning, your life will have an end. Just as the world had a beginning, the world will have an end.

2. There are many differing ideas about the end of the world. Your own views are based upon your *worldview,* your personal belief system.

3. Having a healthy view of the future means that you don't worry about it, but you are prepared for it. In other words, ready, wise, and watchful.

4. There are many signs that point toward the end of the world, but the one thing you can be sure of is this: *The end of the world will occur in your lifetime.*

5. There is a way for you to be prepared for and live through the end of the world with absolute confidence and security. All you have to do is accept the invitation to join Club Forever.

Dig Deeper

Here are several terrific books to start you on your journey to investigate the end of the world:

Understanding the Times by David Noebel. This single volume is worth its weight in gold (which is a lot considering the fact that the book has nearly 900 pages). We haven't found a book that does a better job of explaining the different worldviews.

Christianity 101 by Gilbert Bilezikian. A basic guide to "Eight Basic Christian Beliefs," including a well-written section on the end times.

How to Study Bible Prophecy for Yourself by Tim LaHaye. A simple, reliable book on the basics of Bible prophecy.

Eternity by Joseph Stowell. A good book to get you started thinking about eternity and what it means to your life.

Reason in the Balance by Phillip Johnson. A law professor gives a complete analysis of naturalistic humanism and takes on the "intellectual superstition" of our day.

Moving On . . .

You're probably ready to begin digging into all the interesting details about the end of the world, but we're not quite ready to take you there (you can always skip ahead, but we hope you'll keep reading). As much as possible, we want to show you why you can trust the information coming up in Parts II and III. More importantly, we want you to be sure that your view of the end of the world is based on truth that you have discovered for yourself—not just because we told you.

There's a phrase in our popular culture that has become synonymous with skepticism: *The truth is out there*. We think there's a better phrase, and it comes from the mouth of Jesus Himself: *And you will know the truth, and the truth will set you free*. In a world filled with voices claiming to be the truth, it's important that you discover *true* truth. Get ready, 'cause here it comes.

Chapter 2

Phonies, Flakes, and Experts: Who Do You Trust?

U nreasonable and absurd ways of life . . . are truly an offense to God.

—*William Law*

We can sit here all day (or as long as it takes you to read this book) and give you our view of the end of the world. We can give you our assurance that God is in control, that He has a plan for the world, and that you have a future beyond this life on earth. We can do our best to *convince* you of these things. But you're not going to really believe this stuff unless you investigate it for yourself.

Until you personally look at all of the options out there and make an effort to separate fact from fiction—and faith from fantasy—all of the information in the world isn't going to make a difference in your life.

The bottom line is that you have to *decide for yourself*. Don't let someone else tell you what to believe about your life and where it's headed—because it's *your life*. You are ultimately responsible for making the decisions that affect your life now and forever.

What we want to do in this chapter is lay out the options for you. We want to give you enough information so you can make an intelligent decision. Choose wisely. Your life and your future depend on it.

Bruce & Stan

Chapter 2

Phonies, Flakes, and Experts: Who Do You Trust?

What's Ahead

➤ Your future: the good, the bad, and the ugly
➤ Who do you trust?
➤ The ultimate source: going straight to the Programmer
➤ Examining God's resumé
➤ Putting God to the test

You would think that making a decision about life's most important issue—your eternal future—wouldn't be all that difficult. You would think that the truth would be easy to find. Unfortunately, that isn't the case. It's *very* difficult. The problem isn't the issue itself. It's the number of choices out there! And here's the tricky part: *Only one choice will give you eternal life.*

It's kind of like the scene in the movie *Indiana Jones and the Last Crusade,* where our hero solves the puzzle and gets into the room where the Holy Grail—the cup of Christ—is guarded by an ancient knight. Only there isn't just one cup—there are hundreds. And it's up to Indiana Jones to choose the right one. "Choose wisely," the knight advises.

47

While the movie is fiction, it illustrates a valid point. You've got to choose from hundreds of phony options, all of which are calling out, "Choose me! I've got the answers." You can cover your ears and try to avoid hearing the voices, or you can take responsibility and face up to a very important question:

Who do you trust?

Every river has a source, a beginning. Likewise, every idea and every stream of thought has a source. Someone had to think it first. So as we consider these ideas about the end of the world, we need to look at the sources. We've conveniently divided the sources into three categories.

Your Future: the Good, the Bad, and the Ugly

All streams of thought are not created equal. They range from the normal to the downright bizarre. Let's take a look at these in reverse order.

The Ugly

We're going to start with some very weird—and sometimes dangerous—areas. But we have to deal with these sources, because there are people (more than you think) who base their personal belief systems on them.

The Psychic Network. You may be convinced that the recent phenomenon of psychics on television is nothing more than a clever marketing scheme

"Are Psychics for Real?"

GLAD YOU ASKED

They go by many names: psychics, mediums, astrologers, channelers. And they all have one goal: to convince you that they have supernatural ability to look beyond this world into other worlds. Sometimes they claim to fore-tell the future. So are they all just using smoke and mirrors like a skilled magician, or is their power real? First of all, you should never get close enough to find out. The Bible specifically forbids "fortune-telling" and "witchcraft" (Leviticus 19:26). Second, if the supernat-ural power of these people *is* for real, you can be sure it's not from God. And if it's not from God, it's from the enemy of God—Satan. That may sound a little harsh, but read what John had to say about people who claim to speak by the Spirit:

> *You must test them to see if the spirit they have comes from God. For there are many false prophets in the world. This is the way to find out if they have the Spirit of God: If a prophet acknowledges that Jesus Christ became a human being, that person has the Spirit of God. If a prophet does not acknowledge Jesus, that person is not from God. Such a person has the spirit of the Antichrist* (1 John 4:1-3).

Suddenly these people don't seem so harmless, do they?

designed to bilk a lot of money out of unsuspecting people. We're not about to argue that point. No doubt the psychics and their friends on cable are making good money, but the sad reality is that an increasing number of people seriously buy into this hucksterism and, in fact, shape their lives on the counsel and predictions of these psychics.

Psychics claim to predict the future. Their secret is that they make their "predictions" so general that they could apply to anyone (such as, "You're going to have a new relationship in your future"). Wanting to believe in this secret to knowing the future, people willingly buy into the scheme. As far as these paying customers are concerned, we have to conclude that they are either: a) really desperate or b) genuinely interested in what's going to happen in the future. We suspect it's a little of both.

The occult. This is where psychic parlor games get serious. The little man with the white hair on television may be a harmless actor, but the occult—which focuses on Satan and his world—is very real. Here's what the Bible says about the occult:

> *For we are not fighting against people made of flesh and blood, but against the evil rulers and authorities of the unseen world, against those mighty powers of darkness who rule this world, and against wicked spirits in the heavenly realms* (Ephesians 6:12).

Witchcraft is on the rise and it's everywhere (especially on television and in the movies). Vampire themes are common in books, movies, and fashion.

Several popular rock bands openly promote Satan worship. Contact with "the powers of darkness" gives some people the feeling of power and importance. They may even feel like they have some control over the future. We have only one piece of advice: Stay far away from this stuff. It is not a game. Get it out of your house and turn it off when it comes on your television, even if the witch is a cute teenage girl. This path is a big dead end.

New Agers. You don't hear the term *New Age* as much as you used to, but that's because there are so many different types of people who practice New Age beliefs. They may be into astrology or channeling, or they may have taken the popular "Course in Miracles." Whatever philosophy they believe in, Christian pollster George Barna calls them "New Age Practitioners." He says they share the following characteristics:

- ✓ Faith is a private matter. There's no one right or one wrong way to believe.
- ✓ Religious principles come from a variety of sources, because there's no one authority.
- ✓ The deity you worship is blended with your own self, because you ultimately are striving to be one with the deity.
- ✓ There is more focus on "religious consciousness" than religious practice.

Barna estimates that one in five Americans are New Agers. That means that one in five Americans do not have a definite idea about God, and they are uncertain about the future.

NEW YORK TIMES
BESTSELLERS

In recent years, several of the bestselling books on the *New York Times* book list have dealt with the life beyond and the future.

✓ *The Celestine Prophecy* by James Redfield is a parable about an ancient Peruvian manuscript containing nine insights, which lead to "an exciting new image of human life and a positive vision of how we will save this planet, its creatures, and its beauty." The book has sold more than five million copies. (A sequel, *The Tenth Insight*, deals with the "After Life Dimension.")

✓ *Talking to Heaven* is by James Van Praagh, a self-proclaimed medium who communicates with men, women, children, and animals who have died. He shows "what lies beyond our visible world and answers our most profound questions about life after death." This book sat on top of the *New York Times* bestseller list for months.

✓ *Magical Passes* by Carlos Castaneda encourages the reader to "perceive any of the worlds that exist beside our own" by assuming a series of body positions and physical movements practiced by shamans and sorcerers. The *New York Times* said that "we are incredibly fortunate to have Carlos Castaneda books," which have sold millions over the years.

The Bad

Now we're going to consider some of the more popular sources. We say that because you would be surprised how many people use these to form their beliefs about God and the end of the world.

The media. We're a media-crazy culture. We use the media to entertain us, inform us, and inspire us. And every time we turn on the television, watch a movie, read a newspaper or magazine, log onto the Internet, or even pick up the phone, we are capturing ideas and beliefs about everything from politics to religion. In fact, some people seem unable to form an opinion about life without first seeing what Oprah has to say. And many of us can't make sense of world events until we find out how CNN is reporting them. There's no question that the media is shaping our culture's ideas, especially our ideas about the future.

The tabloids. The supermarket tabloids have been predicting the future for years, even before it was in style (typical headline: "Man Abducted by Aliens Returns to Talk About Judgment Day"). It's goofy stuff, but people read it. And a frightening number actually believe what they read.

It is interesting to note that tabloids love to talk about Judgment Day and the end of the world. We saw a paper recently that gave an actual date when Christ would return, and to give it validity, they put a classic drawing of Jesus on the page. It was pretty weird.

> *A* growing number of intelligent people believe in UFOs and aliens. *USA Today* printed a survey showing that 44 percent of all registered voters believe there is intelligent life on other planets.

Cult of the month. The most recent edition of the *Encyclopedia of American Religions* lists more than 2100 religious groups, ranging from Christianity and Judaism to UFO cults waiting for their eternal rescue by flying saucer. In fact, most of the new religious groups are cults, which means that they use selections from the Bible (ones they like!), along with healthy doses of other belief systems, combining them to create their own strange concoction.

Movie Stars and Yoga

It's amazing how many famous people get caught up in the practice of Eastern religion, which can express itself in a variety of beliefs ranging from the power of yoga to reincarnation. It's not uncommon for celebrities to have personal gurus or spirit "guides," who have assembled their philosophies from the leftover parts of other cults and religions. They also tend to collect a handsome fee for their guidance.

The Good

Now that we've eliminated some of the potential sources for dependable information regarding the end of the world, we are left with a burning question: Where do we look for answers? There are at least three different sources that are reasonably reliable when it comes to building a belief system.

Common sense. This one is pretty important, because when you trust your common sense in the area of belief, you are trusting something God has planted in your very being. From the Bible we know that God has placed in each one of us at least two ideas:

✓ The idea about God

Instead of believing what they knew was the truth about God, they deliberately chose to believe lies. So they worshiped the things God made but not the Creator himself, who is to be praised forever (Romans 1:25).

✓ The idea about eternity

He has made everything beautiful in its time.
He has also set eternity in the hearts of men
(Ecclesiastes 3:11 NIV).

These common-sense ideas about God and eternity
can go a long ways toward shaping your belief in
God. But ultimately your common sense needs to be
verified by objective truth.

History. Now we're getting into an objective, verifiable area of thought and practice. History is basically
the record of human events from the beginning to the
present. History as we know it is also a fairly new
phenomenon (historically speaking, of course). According to scholar Carl F. H. Henry, the ancient world
didn't keep historical records; people simply saw
things happening in "repetitive cycles" or as being
significant only for their particular culture.

By contrast, the Hebrew prophets knew that God acts
and works out His plan in history. They understood
that God, who is eternal, created time and history for
our benefit. He has acted in history in the past, and
He will act in history at some future time to bring
our world to an end. God became a human being and
entered our chronology of time—known as *chronos*,
which describes days, months, and years—in the
form of Jesus. He became a part of human history.

Science and reason. There was a time when the world
thought that science and God were at irreconcilable
odds with each other. Scientists thought that faith in

God had no place in science, and people who had faith in God didn't think they could trust science. In fact, there's been a battle raging between the two for most of this century, and the effect has been to keep the Bible out of the classroom and science out of the church. What a shame.

God created science when He created the world. Science is nothing more than observing what is in the natural world and then drawing conclusions from it. When you look at our world—whether it's through a microscope or a telescope—the intricacies and order of the universe are so compelling that many leading scientists today do not accept the theory that our world came about purely by chance. Instead, the world shows evidence of an intricate design. And if there was a design, there had to be a designer (many scientists aren't ready or willing to draw that conclusion, but that's not because the idea is unreasonable).

Of course, the Bible tells us who that designer is.

The more astronomers learn about the origin and development of the universe, the more evidence they accumulate for the existence of God, and for the God of the Bible in particular.

—Hugh Ross, astrophysicist

From the time the world was created, people have seen the earth and sky and all that God made.

They can clearly see his invisible qualities—his eternal power and divine nature. So they have no excuse whatsoever for not knowing God (Romans 1:20).

As for the end of the world, science now agrees that it is going to happen (remember the Second Law of Thermodynamics?). What science can't do—nor can history or our common sense, for that matter—is tell us what to do when the world does end.

"What If I Take a Little Truth from Each Source?"

Maybe you have no problem throwing out the really bizarre sources—such as the psychics or the occult—but you place a lot of confidence in several of the other sources. In fact, you may be comfortable taking a little truth from each one of them, especially the various cults and religions. "Don't they all contain some truth, and doesn't all truth lead to God?" you might ask.

This practice of picking and choosing beliefs from different sources is called *syncretism*. Although syncretism is inherently illogical (in syncretism you can hold two diametrically opposed ideas at the same time), it's a strong trend among people, even those who claim to be religious. The one true God—the God of Creation and of history—has no place in syncretism, and syncretism will not lead to the one true God and His plan for the future of humankind.

Who Do You Trust?

Sorting out these sources—plus many others we didn't even list—is no easy task. But it must be done for one simple reason: *Your life depends on it!*

A lot of people are willing to give a little thought to the sources for truth about our lives and the future, and there are even those who are willing to give extensive brainpower toward finding the truth. Thinking is good! But even good thinking won't do you any good unless you reach a conclusion as to where your thinking should begin. To put it another way, which truth is really *true?*

Bruce and Stan's Truth Detector

Once again, it's Bruce and Stan to the rescue! We want to give you a "truth detector" to help you come to the right conclusion regarding the truth about God and your future. Here are five questions you should ask about any source of belief before you commit your trust—and your life—to it.

1. Can I verify the source? Can I check the source against other verifiable standards, such as history? Are there people, both in the present and the past, who can testify to its truth?

2. Can I trust the source? Is it completely trustworthy in all situations? Has there ever been a time when the source was not true?

3. Does everyone who goes to the source get the same results? Is the source objective (which means it's the same for everybody) or subjective (which means it's different for everybody)?

4. Does the source come with a guarantee? Is there some way I can know if the source will be true and trustworthy in the future?

5. Would I stake my life on the source? Does my belief in the source and its truth lead me to entrust my life to it—both now and forever?

If you were to put each of the sources for truth we've talked about so far under the scrutiny of Bruce and Stan's truth detector, there's no question that each of them would fail—and fail miserably. Hey, some wouldn't pass *any* of the questions!

So where do you go for truth? (We thought you would never ask.) There's only one source capable of standing up to these questions and any others you could ever think of. There's only one source even worthy of being scrutinized in such a manner. That source isn't an impersonal piece of scientific data, or a clever idea somebody came up with. This source is the ultimate Source, the one true God.

God is the Creator of the universe and all that's in it. Our question should not be, "Does He exist?" but rather, "What is He like?" and "What does He know about my future and the future of the world?"

The Ultimate Source: Going Straight to the Programmer

If you had a question about your computer software program, who would be the best person to ask for an answer? We think you know.

✓ Not the salesman who sold the program to you. (He's a smooth talker, but he doesn't know diddly-squat about programming.)

✔ And not the janitor of the software company. (He is conscientious about his job, but is more experienced with porcelain than programming.)

✔ You would go straight to the programmer who created the software. Who better than the designer to tell you all about it? After all, he knows everything about it.

The same logic applies to finding out about how the world is going to end. You ought to go to the designer/creator of the whole thing. That (in case you haven't made the connection yet) would be God.

Now we don't want you to just blindly accept our suggestion to believe what God says about the end of the world. After all, don't forget that we were the ones who told you that you must decide for yourself. So don't just take our word for it. Check out God's credentials, and then make up your mind.

Examining God's Resumé

Why should you believe what God has to say about the end of the world? Why is God any more trustworthy than Madame Brazieer (the fortune-teller) or Bubba Fletcher (who claims to receive alien telepathic signals through the steel plate in his head)? We don't expect you to trust God just because the coins in our pockets say we do.

You have a right to be skeptical. So let's suppose that you asked God to submit His resumé to prove His credentials as a reliable source for information about the end of the world (and more importantly, as a reliable source for information about what is in store for *your* future). We think the resumé would read something like this:

Name: God

He is known by several other Old Testament names which give a few clues to His expertise as an authority about the future of the world. He is also known as:

✓ Jehovah (a term meaning "I Am that I Am" to indicate that He alone is sufficient for every need, problem, or circumstance);

✓ Elohim (a reference to His power and might);

✓ El-Shaddai (meaning "Almighty"); and

✓ El-Roi (meaning "the strong One who sees everything").

Age: Eternal

God existed before time began. We can't explain it; that is just the way He is. He had no beginning, and He will have no end. He is not defined by time.

> *Before the mountains were created, before you made the earth and the world, you are God, without beginning or end* (Psalm 90:2).

God defies time. He never ages or grows old (Hebrews 1:12).

Residence Address: Heaven

So if you want to know if heaven really exists and what it is like, you might want to listen to the One who created it and lives there (Deuteronomy 26:15).

LIVING IN THE ETERNITY-TIME CONTINUUM

Don't miss this "always existent" aspect of God's nature. He has always existed. He has no beginning or end. His existence is, and always has been, eternal.

> *The eternal God is your refuge, and his everlasting arms are under you* (Deuteronomy 33:27).

This means that *time* is irrelevant to God. So don't be surprised when you read in the Bible that Jesus is going to come back to earth *soon* (and so far "soon" has been almost 2000 years). Since God is living in the eternity-time continuum, His time frame is completely different than ours.

Accomplishments

The resumé could get a little long at this point. Here are just a few of God's accomplishments which are particularly pertinent to your end-of-the-world inquiry:

✓ Created the universe and the earth (Genesis 1:1).

✓ Created light (Genesis 1:3).

✓ Created the human race (Genesis 1:27).

✓ Sustains all life (Psalm 36:9).

✓ Controls nature (Psalm 104).

✓ Commands the weather (Psalm 148:8).

Special Abilities

The list could be endless, but here are three abilities which are especially relevant for anyone who speaks with authority about the future:

- ✓ God sees all things (Proverbs 15:3).
- ✓ God knows the size and scope of the universe (Psalm 147:4).
- ✓ He knows the past, present, and future (Acts 15:18).

Personality Traits

Here is where you are really going to see God's qualifications as an expert about the future:

- ✓ He is infinite (1 Kings 8:27).
- ✓ He is everywhere at the same time ("omnipresent") (Psalm 139:7-12).
- ✓ He is all-powerful ("omnipotent") (Genesis 18:14).
- ✓ He knows everything ("omniscient") (Psalm 139:2-6).
- ✓ He is unchangeable ("immutable") (Hebrews 1:12; 13:8).
- ✓ He is in control of everything ("sovereign") (Isaiah 46:9-11).

References

Finally, no resumé is complete without a list of references. Here are a few endorsements from people who have considered God to be reliable and trustworthy in matters pertaining to the future:

- ✓ "No eye has seen, no ear has heard, and no mind has imagined what God has prepared for those who love him"—the apostle Paul, early Christian missionary.

- ✓ "The celestial order and the beauty of the universe complete to admit that there is some excellent and eternal Being, who deserves the respect and homage of men"—Cicero, Roman philosopher.

- ✓ "The more I know of astronomy, the more I believe in God"—Herber D. Curtis, professor of astronomy, University of Michigan.

- ✓ "God is a scientist, not a magician"—Albert Einstein, genius.

Putting God to the Test

On pages 58-59, we gave you five questions to ask as a "truth detector" to determine the correct source for information about the future. Let's see how God does in relation to that test.

1. Can I verify the source? Yes! God's existence has been verified throughout the ages. God is not some passing fad. We have thousands of people over thousands of years who testify to His existence.

TRYING TO PROVE GOD DOESN'T EXIST CAN BE HAZARDOUS TO YOUR BELIEFS

God is not afraid for you to try and prove He doesn't exist. But be careful. Several renowned atheists set out to do just that, and they became strong believers of God in the process. Perhaps you have heard of:

✓ Lew Wallace (1827-1905). An American military leader and writer. He was a major general in the Civil War, and a member of the military court that tried those accused of conspiring to assassinate Abraham Lincoln. He was an atheist until he really started to investigate the whole God thing. His novel *Ben Hur: A Tale of the Christ* won him a worldwide reputation and was a tribute to the complete turn-around of his beliefs.

✓ C.S. Lewis (1898-1963). An English critic and novelist. He studied at Oxford and was a professor at the University of Cambridge. In the process of trying to disprove the existence of God, he became convinced that God's presence is undeniable. Lewis is now recognized as one of the foremost defenders of Christianity. His books include *The Chronicles of Narnia, The Screwtape Letters* (an allegory in which a senior devil instructs his apprentice nephew devil in methods of moral temptation), and *Mere Christianity* (a defense of the Christian faith).

2. Can I trust the source? Yes! Many people have tried to disprove God's existence, but none have ever succeeded. In fact, some very committed atheists have been persuaded of God's reality as they tried to disprove His existence.

3. Does everyone who goes to the source get the same results? Yes! There is no discrimination with God. He never plays favorites.

God doesn't show partiality (Acts 10:34).

In fact, His love extends to all people everywhere.

He does not want anyone to perish (2 Peter 3:9).

4. Does the source come with a guarantee? Yes, many of them! First, there is a guarantee that you will find God if you sincerely look for Him.

"For I know the plans I have for you," says the LORD. *"They are plans for good and not for disaster, to give you a future and a hope. . . . If you look for me in earnest, you will find me when you seek me"* (Jeremiah 29:11,13).

And it is a lifetime guarantee if you will just believe in Him.

Believe on the Lord Jesus and you will be saved (Acts 16:31).

5. Would I stake my life on the source? That is for you to decide. All we can say is that many people have chosen death rather than forsaking their relationship with God. The apostle Paul said it this way:

For I live in eager expectation and hope that I will never do anything that causes me shame, but that I will always be bold for Christ, as I have been in the past, and that my life will always honor Christ, whether I live or die. For to me, living is for Christ, and dying is even better (Philippians 1:20,21).

So what do you think? Does God pass the test? Do you find Him to be the best—the only—reliable source for information about the future? There are a lot of options out there. Choose carefully. Your life depends on it.

"What's That Again?"

1. You need to carefully consider your source of information about your future and the end of the world.

2. Don't be afraid to use your common sense, history, and science to evaluate these sources of information.

3. Only rely on information about the future which comes from a source that meets the tests of being verifiable, trustworthy, impartial, and guaranteed.

4. Consider how God can satisfy all of the tests as the only reliable source for information about the future. His resumé proves that He is qualified to know about all things—including the events surrounding the end of the world and the specifics about your future.

Dig Deeper

We've covered a lot of ground in this chapter, so the books we're recommending run the gamut from philosophy to aliens:

Love Your God with All Your Mind by J. P. Moreland. A professor of philosophy challenges us to use our minds to further God's kingdom. Intelligent people have a reason to believe in God, and this book shows you why.

Encyclopedia of New Age Beliefs by John Ankerberg and John Weldon. Two experts on New Age practices give a comprehensive overview of the New Age and its spiritual and social significance.

Occult Invasion by Dave Hunt. This thoroughly re-searched book shows how occult beliefs are influ-encing our children, our society, and our government.

Alien Obsession by Ron Rhodes. This fascinating book explores our attraction to the paranormal. Dr. Rhodes speculates that the acceptance of "aliens" is setting the stage for the Antichrist.

Bruce & Stan's Guide to God by (who else?) Bruce Bickel and Stan Jantz. We get to the heart of who God is, where He came from, and how He has set up this world from beginning to end. We like it, and we think you will, too.

Moving On . . .

Perhaps you are inclined to believe that God is the best choice to answer your questions about the future. So what do you do next? How do you access all of what He knows? It's not like He has a web site from which you can download everything you ever wanted to know about the end of the world.

Well, God may not have a web site, but that doesn't mean you can't find what He says on the Internet. It is there (and other places, too). Everything God wants you to know about your future and the end of the world is in the Bible. Whether you pull the Bible off the shelf, listen to it on an audiotape, or read it on your computer screen, the message is God's Word to you.

In the next chapter, we'll show you that the Bible is not just an outdated collection of ancient religious manuscripts written by a bunch of gray-bearded Jewish shepherds. Quite the contrary. The Bible contains the very words of God, written for you, to reveal the blueprints of His plans for you and the rest of the human race. So if you want to know what God says about the end of the world, the Bible is the place to look.

Chapter 3

The Bible:
God's Handbook for the Past, Present, and Future

An aged grandfather explained why he read the Bible several hours every day: *You might say I am cramming for my final examination.*

God could have chosen many different ways to communicate with us.

✔ He could have used skywriting—scrawling the words across the horizon in the clouds. This would have made it convenient for the world to read, except on a windy day.

✔ He could have bellowed His message in a thunderous voice from the heavens loud enough for the entire world to hear (but with the different time zones, some people would always be startled awake in the middle of their night's sleep).

✔ He could have simply programmed electronic impulses in our heads (the sacred equivalent to zapping your brain with a cattle prod).

But He didn't choose any of these methods. Instead, He chose something very simple, but very effective: a book.

The Bible is the only book of its kind. It is the bestselling book of all time, and for good reason: It contains the very words of God. In your quest to find out what God says about the end of the world, the Bible is your best resource.

In this chapter we will present evidence which substantiates our claim that the Bible contains God's message about your future. But the Bible is more than just a book about the end of the world. It also explains God's entire plan for the human race—from beginning to end—and in this chapter we'll cover it all for you. If you think this is a lot to cover in one chapter, you're right! But what we have attempted to do is to compact all of time, from eternity past to eternity future, into less than 3600 words.

Bruce & Stan

Chapter 3

The Bible:
God's Handbook for the Past, Present, and Future

What's Ahead

- When God spoke, who was listening?
- So many pages, and no mistakes?
- It helps to know the beginning before the end
- Part One—eternity past: an ill-fated intergalactic insurrection
- Part Two—eternity present: Bruce and Stan's brief history of the human race
- Part Three—eternity future: the end is only the beginning
- If you only remember one thing, remember this

*W*e imagine that you are anxious to hear what God has said about how the world is going to end. After all, as we discussed in chapter 2, God is the best source for information about the future. And God has said quite a lot about the events that will occur at the end of the world. Too bad you weren't around several thousand years ago when He said them.

But don't be discouraged that you were born several millennia too late. God has gone to great effort to make sure that His message was recorded and

73

preserved for you—for you to read at your own convenience in your own moment in time.

In this chapter we will give you an overview of God's entire plan for the world—from the past, to the present, and into the future. We'll be getting our information directly from the Bible, so before we begin with our synopsis, we want to reassure you that the Bible is God's own handbook.

When God Spoke, Who Was Listening?

In *Bruce and Stan's Guide to the End of the World,* most of the information we're going to give you comes directly from the Bible. So it's very important that your confidence in the Bible is reasonably high. In fact, we think you should put your *complete* trust in the Bible as the authoritative and totally dependable Word of God.

It's God's Book and It's God's Word

We've already said that the Bible is the world's most unique book. Here's why. *The Bible is God's revelation of Himself to people.* That means God has told us about Himself and His plan for the world in the pages of the Bible.

We want to be very clear about this. The Bible isn't just a story *about* God. Neither is the Bible someone's best guess about who God is and what He has done. Instead, the Bible is God's personal message to us. It's a divine letter (a long one, we admit) written to every person born into the human race (and unless we're terribly mistaken, that includes you).

Since the Bible contains the very words of God, you don't have to *wonder* about God. You can *know* about God's plan for you and the world because He has left us a message. When you read the Bible, it's as if God is talking directly to you.

> *You accepted what we said as the very word of God—which, of course, it was. And this word continues to work in you who believe* (1 Thessalonians 2:13).

So How Did God Do It?

Here's an amazing question to ponder. Just how did God, who is Spirit (that is, no flesh and blood), put His words into a format that we flesh-and-blood humans can read and understand? In a word, God *spoke* the Bible into existence in much the same way as He created the universe.

> *By faith we understand that the entire universe was formed at God's command, that what we now see did not come from anything that can be seen* (Hebrews 11:3).

In other words, He did it by literally *breathing* His words *into* more than 40 different writers over a 1500-year time period. That's what it means when you hear that the Bible has been *inspired* by God. *Inspire* literally means "to breathe or blow into."

> *All Scripture is inspired by God and is useful to teach us what is true and to make us realize what is wrong in our lives. It straightens us out and teaches us to do what is right* (2 Timothy 3:16).

God's breath gives life. The Bible tells us that when
God created the first man, Adam, He formed his
body from the dust of the ground and "breathed into
it the breath of life." In the same way, when God
breathed into the human authors of the Bible, He
gave *life* to His Word. Because of this process, you
can have complete trust in the Bible, whether it's
talking about history or the way you should live
your life. God, who is perfect, used a foolproof
means to get His message into print: He "breathed
in" what He wanted. Nothing more, nothing less.

So Many Pages, and No Mistakes?

It's one thing to understand how the Bible got from
God to the human authors. The next question you
might be asking is this: "How did the Bible get from
those guys who first wrote it down to us today?" and
"Can we trust the Bible we have today?"

The Test of Truth

First, each of the 66 books in your Bible had to measure up to a set of strict guidelines to determine
which books were God-inspired and which ones
weren't. This process, called *canonization*, was carried
out by a series of church councils in the first few centuries after Christ lived on the earth. Their main task
was to evaluate books written during and after the
time of Christ (the Old Testament *canon* had already
been determined by this time).

Dr. Norman Geisler, our favorite authority on the
Bible, lists five checkpoints these councils used:

1. Does it speak with God's authority?
2. Is it written by a man of God speaking to us as a prophet of God?
3. Does it have the authentic stamp of God?
4. Does it impact us with the power of God?
5. Was it accepted by the people of God?

A key point to remember is that the canon councils did not *declare* a book to be from God. They simply *recognized* the divine authority that was already there. The total canon of Scripture—all 66 books of the Bible—was recognized as the authoritative Word of God by the fourth century A.D.

Write This Down, and Don't Make Any Mistakes

In his excellent book *A Ready Defense*, Josh McDowell asks a very important question: "Since we do not have the original documents [of Scripture], how reliable are the copies we have?" The short answer is that the copies we have are the most reliable of any document ever written.

More copies of Bible manuscripts exist than for any other ancient book (more than 5000 Greek manuscripts of the New Testament alone). And these copies have been declared historically reliable by hundreds of experts ranging from archaeologists to theologians. Here's what Dr. Clark Pinnock, one of the foremost authorities on ancient manuscripts, has to say about the Bible:

There exists no document from the ancient world witnessed by so excellent a set of textual and historical testimonies and offering so superb an array of historical data on which an intelligent decision may be made. An honest [person] cannot dismiss a source of this kind. Skepticism regarding the historical credentials of Christianity is based upon an irrational bias.

You Can Trust the Bible

There's no question that the Bible is the Word of God. Josh McDowell argues that only God could have created a book which:

✓ Has been transmitted accurately from the time it was originally written,

✓ Is correct when it deals with historical people and events,

✓ Contains no "scientific absurdities," and

✓ Remains true and relevant to all people for all time.

Therefore, you can read the Bible with confidence. Even if you don't understand everything (none of us do), you can trust the Bible to deal with you honestly. And you can trust it to speak about our world—from eternity past to eternity future—in a way that's meaningful and true.

So hang on to your hat. Make sure your tray is stowed and your seat is in its upright and locked position. We are going to race through God's plan for the ages as presented in the Bible. As far as we know, no one's ever tried this before, and we recommend that you don't try it at home. We do suggest that you pray and ask God to open your eyes to the wonders of His plan.

It Helps to Know the Beginning Before the End

The end of the world is not going to happen by accident. It will occur according to God's detailed and

---

"What? When? and Why?"

As you read the rest of this chapter, three questions may occur to you:

1. *What is going to happen at the end of the world?* This one we will answer, at least in general terms. This chapter will give you an overview, and we talk about some of the specific topics in chapters 6-10.

2. *When is the end of the world going to occur?* Here's the answer: in the future. (Sorry, that is all you are going to get out of us this early in the book.)

3. *Why is the world going to end like this?* This is one of our favorite questions. The answer can be found in God's plan for mankind. It all has to do with God's love for humanity, humanity's rebellion and rejection of God, and God's efforts to restore that broken relationship.

preordained plan. He has had this plan in operation for centuries, and everything is taking place according to His schedule as it is outlined in the Bible. Now, we could jump directly to a review of what the Bible says about how the world is going to end. But you might feel deprived if we only told you the end of God's plan without explaining the first part.

We want you to know more than just the *what* of the end times. We also want you to know the *why*. That level of understanding is necessary for the future decisions you must make about how you are going to fit in the end-of-the-world scenario.

Our editor said we could only have 23 pages for this chapter, and we have already used up 10 of them, so we are going to have to rip through history at a pretty fast pace. Don't worry, we won't leave out any of the essentials. And don't feel shortchanged, because the major topics of the end times are discussed in more detail in later chapters. Our purpose here is simply to put the whole thing together, from beginning to end, in one package.

It is a fairly ambitious task to cover all of time in just a few pages. Like eating an elephant, we have decided to do it in three large servings, with a lot of little bites in each serving. We'll cover the Bible as if there were three parts to God's handbook. Part One will cover what happened before the human race existed. Part Two will cover the human race from Adam and Eve until now (but we won't be mentioning everyone by name). And Part Three will cover the events of the end of the world. Each part is a very important section of the handbook, so please don't doze off.

Part One—Eternity Past: An Ill-Fated Intergalactic Insurrection

Before God created the earth and people, He created angels. He gave these celestial beings the freedom of choice because He didn't want a bunch of prepro-grammed robots. Everything was going along great in heaven until one of the high-ranking angels, Lucifer, attempted to lead a palace revolt against God. (Now, we know that Lucifer is shrewd, but his ultimate stupidity is revealed when he attempted a coup against the all-powerful God. His rebellion was doomed from the start.)

THE ORIGINAL STAR WARS

Ever since he was kicked out of heaven, Satan has been at war with God. He knows he is the biggest loser of all time, but he doesn't want to go down quietly. All of the events of the end of the world are integrally connected with the contin-uing rebellion (and eventual punishment) of Satan, the angels who were court-martialed with him (now known as demons), and all of the members of the human race who got sucked into his fraudulent scam.

God squelched the ill-fated rebellion and expelled Lucifer (also known as Satan) and his fellow celestial chumps out of heaven. The ultimate punishment for their treason would come later. In the meantime, they were roaming around with no place to go.

Part Two—Eternity Present: Bruce and Stan's Brief History of the Human Race

No one knows how much time passed during the gap between Part One and Part Two. It doesn't really matter. But as the page is turned for Part Two, God created our universe. After creating the solar systems and the earth (with vegetation and animals), God specifically designed a man. The Bible says that God made man in His own image. This doesn't mean that God has ten toes and chest hair. The "image of God" which was placed in man was a "soul"—an eternal nature. So every member of the human race has a mind, a body, and a soul (or spirit). Even after our death and the deterioration of our mind (which for some of us happens sooner than death) and body, our soul lives on forever.

God began the human race with Adam and Eve. They were living the ideal life in the Garden of Eden. They had a personal friendship with God (and it's a pretty good situation when your best friend is the almighty Creator of the universe). Life was perfect.

YES VIRGINIA, THERE IS LIFE AFTER DEATH!

This concept is HUGE. It is what makes the end of the world stuff directly relevant and intimately personal to YOU regardless of whether or not you die before the world comes to an end. Because ultimately you will never die. Your soul/spirit lives on forever. This is the "life after death" question that everyone wonders about. But that question is a no-brainer. The more pertinent question is, Where will you spend eternity after the world has come to an end? There are only two sections: smoking and nonsmoking. But wait! We're getting ahead of ourselves.

But then Satan snuck in. He knew that God had designed humanity with a free will (Adam and Eve were capable of either obeying or disobeying God's instructions). God had laid down a few simple instructions for them to follow, but instead of doing what God had asked, Adam and Eve chose to believe Satan's lies. They blatantly disobeyed God, and everything was ruined. The Bible calls their disobedience "sin." Sin is such an insidious virus that it infected them and all of their descendants—the whole human race. Since Adam and Eve, every person has been born with a sin nature.

"What's So Bad About Sin?"

Sin is so bad because God is so holy. He cannot tolerate sin of any kind because He is perfect. This is a difficult concept for us to grasp because we can't comprehend how righteous God is. But the Bible makes it clear that sin is so bad that:

✔ It has infected all of us. (*For all have sinned*—Romans 3:23.)

✔ As rebellion against God, it deserves the same eternal death penalty imposed on Satan. (*For the wages of sin is death*—Romans 6:23.)

Don't think for a moment that you are innocent and are being unfairly incriminated and convicted by Adam and Eve's sin. You have plenty of your own (lies, anger, cheating, etc.), and it only takes one to violate God's standard of holiness.

God is not a mean, old ogre who is pleased to see His creations doomed to eternal punishment. Just the opposite. Even though the human race has continued Adam and Eve's example of rejecting God and rebelling against His authority, God still longs to restore a personal relationship with the human race. Unfortunately, under God's divine design, sin can only be forgiven by the death of an innocent person, and there has never been a human being who could qualify.

But God Himself had the solution to mankind's sin problem. His only Son, Jesus, would come to earth as a man to die as a sacrifice for mankind—dying in our place so we don't have to suffer eternal punishment. That was the whole purpose of Jesus Christ being on earth. His crucifixion was not a colossal mistake which ruined God's plan. Quite the contrary. God's plan was fulfilled exactly. Jesus was born to die so that we might live.

Chapter 11

Remember the "free will" which God has given to us? Well, that freedom of choice still applies. In the almost 2000 years since Jesus died, rose from the dead, and then went back to heaven, human beings continue to have the opportunity to accept or reject the sacrifice Jesus made on our behalf. What Jesus did on the cross was enough to "save" us from eternal punishment, but we must decide whether or not we want to accept this "salvation." We accept salvation by giving God the priority He deserves in our lives. (There will be more about "salvation" in

---

CHRISTIANITY: TO BE OR NOT TO BE?

Is the subject of "Christianity" relevant to the end of the world? You bet it is. Some of the events at the end of the world will affect everyone. But some apply only to Christians, and others apply only to people who have not accepted Jesus Christ's gift of salvation. Your ultimate destination for eternity will be determined by whether or not you are a Christian.

chapter 11.) Those who accept God's gift are referred to as "Christians" (which means a follower of Christ).

Part Three—Eternity Future: the End Is Only the Beginning

Here it is! This is what you have been waiting for. Part Three of God's handbook—what the Bible says about how the world is going to end. Before we get started, you should know that some people say the page has already been turned to start Part Three. Others say we are still living in Part Two. There is ambiguity about this because the Bible uses a lot of symbolism to describe the events of the end of the world (which we'll discuss in chapter 5).

Despite the ambiguity and symbolism, the Bible describes some clear and definite events that will be easily recognizable and undeniable as the world comes near its end. Until they actually happen, however, scholars are not agreed on their sequential order. We'll talk more about the different views and timetables in chapters 6-10. For now let's just look briefly at the events and aspects of the "end of the world" about which most Bible scholars agree:

Return of Jesus Christ. Jesus already invaded planet Earth once—2000 years ago when He was born as a baby and crucified as a man. He's coming back again in the future. This "second coming of Christ" is the pivotal part of God's divine design for humanity. But it won't happen with the obscurity that accompanied the birth of Christ in Bethlehem. In startling contrast, the return of Christ will be marked by much fanfare, which all the inhabitants of the earth will witness. The return of Christ will be closely associated with world turmoil and calamity. There will be natural disasters of unprecedented proportions. A treacherous world politician will intentionally initiate global warfare.

Immortal soul. Every person has a spiritual dimension that lives forever. There is life beyond the grave.

Future bodily resurrection. At some point in the future, the immortal souls of all people will be given new bodies. The dead will be "resurrected" at God's appointed time, and all people, from all of human history, will be outfitted with a new body for eternity.

Final judgment. Every person who ever lived, along with Satan and his demons, will at one future date stand before God. There will be no exceptions.

Eternity forever in one place or the other. Sometimes people refer to the reward of believing in Christ as "eternal life." That reference is slightly imprecise. All of us, because of our "spirit" nature, will have eternal life. It's just a question of whether you will spend eternity in the "smoking" or "nonsmoking" section. (Finally, we get to this.) The Bible refers to hell and heaven as real places. Very real. We'll describe hell in chapter 9 (it will be a hell of a discussion), and we'll talk about heaven in chapter 10.

If You Only Remember One Thing, Remember This

Well, we made it, and so did you. From eternity past to eternity future in 8 pages. That's a lot to absorb, so you may want to take a rest until the pressure subsides in your cranial capillaries. In fact, you may want to read this chapter again just to reinforce your understanding of the events we've discussed.

We have given you a lot of information, but you don't have to remember all of it. (You can always come back later and look up what you forget.) However, there is one important principle which you should never forget:

You cannot control or escape the events or timing of the end of the world. These things are going to happen, and there is nothing you can do to change them. However, you have control over the destination where you will spend eternity. If you accept salvation through Jesus Christ, you will be choosing heaven. On the other hand, hell is what people choose if they reject Jesus.

BRUCE AND STAN'S
TOP TEN TERMS FOR THE FUTURE

We'll give you more specifics in subsequent chapters, but here is a short list of "end times" terminology for the Bible's outline of the future, presented in alphabetical order:

Antichrist: Like a ventriloquist uses a dummy, Satan is going to get a political leader under his control. This world leader, referred to in the Bible as the Antichrist, will be used by Satan to achieve his evil purposes as the world comes to an end. The Antichrist will be aided and abetted by his cohort in crime, the false prophet, who will be able to perform miracles through satanic power.

Armageddon: This battle will be the last world war, and it will be worse than all previous wars combined. A coalition of nations under the leadership of the Antichrist will prepare for battle against a 200-million-soldier army from the east.

Great White Throne Judgment: This is the scary one! All people from throughout history who rejected God and His Son, Jesus, will be brought to this judgment. The outcome of each judgment is a foregone conclusion. Their sins will not have been forgiven because of their unbelief. As a result, their punishment will be the same as that of Satan and his demons: torture in hell forever and ever.

Heaven: Heaven is not a mere fantasy. It is real. There are over 500 references in the Bible to heaven, and it is called "the abode of God." Descriptions include streets of gold, mansions, and the absence of any pain or sorrow. It's greatest defining characteristic is that it is the place where God dwells, and to live in heaven for eternity means that you will be in the presence of God forever.

Hell: Hell is a place of eternal torture and suffering. The punishment is real. The greatest defining characteristic of hell is that it represents total and complete separation from God.

Judgment Seat of Christ: This judgment is reserved for people who believed in Jesus. It is not a proceeding to determine guilt or innocence. (Remember: Everyone who believes

in Christ receives forgiveness for their sins—so they are automatically declared "not guilty.") Instead, this is a judgment
where God gives rewards for faithful service to Him.

Millennium: The millennium (properly referred to as the "millennial kingdom") is a period of a thousand years when there
will be peace on earth. Christ will reign as King in all His
splendor and glory. This will be a time of peace, prosperity, and
spiritual renewal such as the world has never known. At the
end of this thousand years, Satan will be released from captivity and make one last, desperate effort to sway human allegiance and seize the throne of Christ. His rebellion will fail,
and he will be thrown into hell's lake of fire forever.

Rapture: At an unknown time, Jesus Christ is going to appear
in the sky and all Christians, living and dead, will be trans-
ported to meet Him in the sky. All of this will happen in the
time it takes for an eye to blink.

Second Coming: As the great battle of Armageddon is about
to begin, Jesus Christ will return to earth to take His place as
the rightful King. Somehow, the battling armies will join
forces to oppose God, but Christ will have with Him all of
the armies of heaven. Christ and His army of angelic hosts
will prevail against the armies of the earth. The Antichrist
and the false prophet will be captured and cast into hell.
Satan and his demons will be bound and gagged for the du-
ration of the millennium.

Tribulation: The Great Tribulation is believed to be a seven-
year period which will have calamities and catastrophes
greater than the world has ever known. Some will be natural
disasters, and others will be caused by mankind. Earthquakes, floods, disease, warfare, and persecution will mark
this time. Planet Earth will not be a preferred vacation spot.
It is believed that all of these events will cause people to

believe in God. The Great Tribulation will have two distinct halves. For the first 3½ years, there will be relative peace and harmony on the earth (except for the natural disasters). But this peace will be an illusion created by the Antichrist. The second 3½ year period will be disastrous for everyone as the Antichrist commences a campaign of horrors.

"What's That Again?"

1. The Bible is the Word of God. God directed the authors to write His message. God's plan for the future of your life and the entire world is recorded in the Bible.

2. The Bible is without error. All its statements are true. You can trust what it says about your life and the world.

3. The end of the world will not happen by accident. From before the beginning of time, God had a plan.

4. God's divine design for humanity revolves around His desire to restore a personal relationship with us. Our sin has cut us off from God, but our sin can be forgiven by belief in Jesus Christ.

5. Within each of us there is a spiritual dimension. Our "soul" is eternal and will live beyond our death. The events at the end of the world include a "resurrection" of our new body.

6. Belief in Jesus is the determining factor for our future. When the world comes to an end, our destination for eternity will be determined by whether we believed in Jesus during our lifetime.

Dig Deeper

There's no substitute for reading the Bible, but it's also a good idea to read some books *about* the Bible. Here are some of our favorites:

What If the Bible Had Never Been Written? by D. James Kennedy. This fascinating book demonstrates that the Bible is the most influential book in history. Dr. Kennedy gives numerous examples of how the Bible has impacted government, laws, and morals.

Bruce and Stan's Guide to the Bible by Bruce Bickel and Stan Jantz. We not only tell you what's in the Bible, but we also tell you why you should read the Bible (hint: It has to do with God). We think you should buy this book!

A Ready Defense by Josh McDowell. One of our favorites, this book is a detailed and well-documented reference work that belongs on your bookshelf. The section on the reliability of the Bible is superb.

Foundations of the Christian Faith by James Montgomery Boice. Here's another book of theology, and the reason we like it is because it is organized chronologically from the beginning to the end of time. The section on the Bible is excellent, and the section on the end of the world is well worth reading.

Moving On . . .

Are you ready to start examining the Bible to see what it says about your future and the end of the world? We hope so, but we must offer a word of caution. We'll give it to you through an analogy.

Have you ever watched a movie when the theater projectionist got the reels out of order? You actually saw all of the movie, but it probably didn't make any sense. Perhaps the storyline seemed confused to you, and most likely you felt disoriented. While you *saw* what was happening, you didn't *understand* it.

A similar feeling could overwhelm you when you read the Bible. You see, the Bible passages about the end of the world are not in sequential order, and they are not all grouped together. You can read what's in the Bible, but trying to understand it may be as confusing as watching that jumbled-up movie. If you've tried reading any of the Bible's prophecies about the end of the world, you know exactly what we mean.

Beginning with the next chapter, we'll try to help you get some sense of orientation; we'll explain the layout of the Bible's predictions about the future. Then in chapter 5 we'll talk about the bizarre symbolism and ambiguous descriptions which leave room for a range of interpretations. In other words, in chapters 4 and 5 we'll try to label the reels so you can make sense out of the movie (because we don't want you to miss the surprise ending).

PART II:

I CAN READ WHAT THE BIBLE SAYS . . . NOW TELL ME WHAT IT MEANS!

> We should all be concerned about the future because we will have to spend the rest of our lives there.
>
> —*Charles Kettering*

As we begin Part II of this book, let's take a quick look at where we've been. (After all, this book is a *guide*.)

✓ *Chapter 1:* All of this business about the end of the world is important and relevant because your life is involved.

✓ *Chapter 2:* The best source of information about the future is God, since we are living under His grand plan.

✓ *Chapter 3:* If you want to know about God's plan for the end of the world, you will find it in the Bible.

Okay. So far, so good. But now we're ready to move to the next step: reading the Bible.

Perhaps you tried reading the Bible before and were frustrated in your attempts to understand what it says about the future. Well, join the club. Reading the Bible is easy, but *understanding* the Bible is not so simple.

If you have never read the Bible before, or if you are having a difficult time figuring out how all of the Bible prophecies about the future fit together, this chapter is for you. We'll show you that there is a sensible arrangement and pattern to the Bible's discussion of the future. When we are finished, many of the prophecies will still seem strange and obscure, but that is the subject of chapter 5. For now, our goal is to help you understand how the various prophecies fit into the overall design of the Bible.

Bruce & Stan

Chapter 4

Reading the Bible for Fun and Prophet

*I*magine you are lost in a foreign city. You feel helpless and confused. You ask strangers for directions to your hotel, but no one speaks English. Out of pity for your situation, someone hands you a map. Now you have the precise directions for your destination. But wait! You still aren't going anywhere! The map is in an unfamiliar foreign language. You recognize the name of the hotel on the map, but there is no "you are here" arrow to identify your current location. There are hundreds of streets on the map, but you might have already passed the one you need, and the streets you are looking at might be scenic detours rather than part of the correct route. Looking at this map isn't getting you anywhere. For all you know, you might be holding it upside down!

For many of us, reading the prophecies from the Bible is like trying to read that map. We know there is accurate information on the page, but it does us little good because we are completely disoriented. We want to know about our final destination, but we can't even figure out where our current location ("the present") fits into the Bible's map of the future. Like all the streets which aren't part of the direct route, we aren't sure which prophecies are scenic detours that have nothing to do with where we want to end up.

If you identify with what we are talking about, then you're probably jumping up and down on the sofa in joyous confirmation that someone else shares your frustration. If you don't have a clue about what we mean, here are a few examples:

✓ How come some of the prophecies about the end of the world are in the *Old* Testament and some are in the *New* Testament? Do the New Testament ones revoke and replace the Old Testament ones? Wouldn't we be better off relying on the most recent ones and rejecting the old, moldy ones?

✓ In Psalm 22, the coming Messiah is described as a dusty shepherd who attends to his smelly sheep. In Psalm 24, the coming Messiah is portrayed as a conquering king who parades in majesty before his adoring subjects. The two descriptions couldn't be more opposite. What gives?

✓ Some of the Old Testament prophets did pretty weird stuff. (Isaiah walked around naked, Hosea married a prostitute, and Ezekiel ate meals cooked over a manure barbecue.) Shouldn't such behavior cause us to question their mental stability and the reliability of their predictions?

✓ Some prophets, like Daniel in the Old Testament and John in the New Testament, made predictions about the future based on elaborate and bizarre dreams which God revealed to them. Other prophets gave predictions based on what God told them. Do the "audio only" versions of prophecy deserve as much credence as the "technicolor" ones?

✓ A bunch of the Old Testament prophets said that the temple in Jerusalem would be rebuilt, but Jesus said the temple would be destroyed. Which is it?

✓ The New Testament writers talk about Jesus coming back to earth right away. Well, since they said it, the stopwatch had been ticking for almost 2000 years. What's with that?

These are just a few prophetical conundrums that occur to us. We think you get the point.

Chapter 5

And then there is the whole subject of how to *interpret* the symbolism of the prophecies. For example, does a reference to a "four-headed beast" refer to a monster with four faces, or is it a primitive description of a military tank with headlights and fog lamps? We'll tackle the subject of interpretation in chapter 5. For now, let's just focus on the context in which the prophecies were made. To start with, let's see if we can put a few labels on the map of biblical prophecy so we can tell which end is up.

Can We Skip It if We Don't Understand It?

If you're like us, confusion and frustration about how Bible prophecy fits together might tempt you to chuck the whole subject and move on to something that can be understood without burning out your brain cells—like the story of David and Goliath. Well, resist that urge, because God had some great reasons for putting prophecies about the future in the Bible.

Getting Face-to-Face with Your Future

Are you worried or anxious about the future? Well, you don't have to be, because you can know your ultimate destiny. The study of Bible prophecy can tell you what's in store for you at the end of your life. Think about it. If you know how things are going to end, you can make the necessary plans. You'll live with more confidence and have a better perspective on life.

> *"For I know the plans I have for you," says the Lord. "They are plans for good and not for disaster, to give you a future and a hope"* (Jeremiah 29:11).

Prophecy is a statement made by God, through a human spokesman (the "prophet"). The proclamation of the prophet falls into one of two categories. Either it is a message expressing one of God's principles for living (referred to as "forthtelling"), or it is a prediction of a future event ("foretelling"). In a discussion about the events of the end of the world, *prophecy* always refers to predicting the events of the future.

Getting Personal with God

Besides helping you know your own future, the study of Bible prophecy can give you a better understanding of who God is. When you realize that about 2000 prophecies in the Bible have been fulfilled, you'll have a keener appreciation of the fact that God is all-knowing. The fulfillment of these Bible predictions shows conclusively that God knows the future as well as the past. If God knows both ends of the time continuum, then you can trust His direction and guidance for your life. After all, He knows everything about you, including the very details of what life has in store for you.

> *Not even a sparrow, worth only half a penny, can fall to the ground without your Father knowing it. And the very hairs on your head are all numbered. So don't be afraid; you are more valuable to him than a whole flock of sparrows* (Matthew 10:29-31).

And That's Not All

But learning about your future and learning about God are not the only benefits. If you stick with the study of this subject, you'll know more about:

World events. Many prophecies affect the world as a whole. The events surrounding the end of the world describe alliances among nations and wars between peoples. A key player in the end times will be the nation of Israel because God has a special plan for His chosen people. A study of prophecy will give you greater insight into what is currently happening in the Middle East and around the world.

Life after death. Everyone is interested in whether there is life after death, but few people want to do what it takes to find out. The Bible teaches that there is an eternal nature in every person—a *spirit* nature that lives on after physical death. A basic understanding of Bible prophecy will answer your questions on this topic.

Angels and demons. There are alien beings in our atmosphere who are actively engaged in spiritual warfare, and you are the battlefield. You'll find out what is going on as you study prophecy.

History. Understanding Bible prophecy can help us understand what has happened in history. Sure, the history textbooks can describe *what* has happened, but reading ancient Bible prophecies can explain *why* it happened.

Reading the Bible Map of Prophecy

The Bible was written over a span of 1500 years by more than 40 different authors. But the Bible is not merely a collection of random religious writings. It is a single volume with a central theme running throughout its pages: God's plan for the human race.

There are two major divisions in the Bible: the Old Testament (writings *before* the birth of Jesus Christ), and the New Testament (those written *after* Jesus was on earth). The Bible contains a lot of prophecy (about one-fourth of the Bible was prophetic at the time it was originally written), but it includes much more than just future predictions. Here is how it breaks down:

Old Testament

There are 39 books in the Old Testament. While there are prophetic references spread throughout the entire Old Testament, most of them occur (not surprisingly) in the books written by the prophets.

Books of beginnings *(Genesis-Deuteronomy).* The first five books of the Bible report how things began: the beginning of the world; the creation of the human race; how sin came into the world; and God's plan to use the Jews (the descendants of Abraham, later known as the nation of Israel) as His "chosen people" to bring His plan of salvation to the world.

Books of history *(Joshua-Esther).* These 12 books review the history of the people of Israel. When they followed God's guidance, things went well. When

The timeline of the Old Testament stops here. The next two sections include books which were mostly written *during* the time covered by the books of history (about 1400 B.C. to 400 B.C.).

they tried to do things their own way, they always got in trouble.

Books of poetry and wisdom *(Job-Song of Songs).* These books include poetry from David (the shepherd boy who became a king), wise sayings from King Solomon, and the story of the sufferings of Job.

Books of prophecy *(Isaiah-Malachi).* These 17 books are all written by Old Testament prophets. Some are called "major prophets" and the rest are referred to as "minor prophets." These designations have nothing to do with the relative importance of the prophets or the accuracy of their predictions. They are purely a reflection of the length of the books they wrote: The major prophets wrote long books; the minor prophets, short ones.

New Testament

There are 27 books in the New Testament. The last book consists entirely of a prophecy of future events, but the other books also contain predictions about events that will occur at the end of the world. Here is how the books can be divided:

Clues You Can Use

Here is what you need to know to understand the writings of the Old Testament prophets.

✓ The writings of the prophets occurred during a 500-year period from about 930 B.C. to 430 B.C.

✓ During this time, a civil war divided the nation of Israel into the northern kingdom (called "Israel") and the southern kingdom (called "Judah").

✓ The Jews were "on again/off again" in their allegiance to God. It was the role of the prophets to encourage the people to turn back to God, warning of invasion and capture by other kingdoms if they failed to do so.

✓ The northern kingdom was captured by the Assyrians in 722 B.C. and the southern kingdom was invaded and captured by the Babylonians in 586 B.C. These were bleak days for the Jews. Their rebellion against God had left them defeated and dejected.

✓ Some of the prophets wrote before the invasions. Some wrote to the Jews in exile. Others wrote to the few Jews who were left behind in Jerusalem, which had been destroyed by the invaders.

✓ Some of the prophets' predictions were short-term warnings (as when Jeremiah predicted that the southern kingdom would be carried away into Babylonian captivity if the Jews didn't return to God—Jeremiah 13:19).

✓ Other predictions were intended to give long-range hope to the Jews that God had not welched on His promise to Abraham that He would make the Jews into a great nation. These prophecies focus on God's promise to send a "Messiah" who would establish His kingdom on earth and rescue the Jews from persecution.

Biographies about Jesus (Matthew-John). These four books, called the "Gospels," give biographical accounts of the life of Christ for the 33-year period from His birth through His crucifixion and resurrection, and His return back to heaven. They cover both the events of the life of Christ and His teachings. Christ often spoke of what would happen at the end of the world. These books are integrally tied into the writings of the Old Testament prophets because the Gospels show that Jesus fulfilled the prophecies about the identity of the Messiah.

Action adventure about the beginning of Christianity (Acts). This book starts with the return of Christ to heaven, and then explains what happened to the people who believed that Jesus was the promised Messiah. These "followers" of Christ formed the first group of Christians. The Book of Acts shows how the message of Christ spread around the world in a few short years, with groups of believers ("churches") springing up in cities throughout the Mediterranean region.

Personal correspondence (Romans-Jude). Twenty-one books (called "epistles") in the New Testament are really letters (remember, these were the days before the phone, fax, and e-mail). The apostles served as mentors to the growing Christian churches and wrote these letters to give the local churches encouragement and instruction for living a life in the pattern of Jesus. Frequently, the teaching about God included references to what would happen at death and the end of the world. These early Christians suffered

"Who Is That Messiah Man?"

Here is a list of some of the Old Testament prophecies about the identity of the Messiah which were fulfilled by Jesus (hundreds of years after the prophecies were made).

Clue to Messiah's Identity	Old Testament Prophecy	Fulfilled by Jesus
Born of a virgin	Isaiah 7:14	Matthew 1:22,23
Born in town of Bethlehem	Micah 5:2	Matthew 2:5,6; Luke 2:4-6
Lived in Egypt for a while	Numbers 24:8; Hosea 11:1	Matthew 2:15
Massacre of infants in His birthplace	Jeremiah 31:15	Matthew 2:17,18
Would heal people	Isaiah 53:4	Matthew 8:16,17
Would teach in parables	Isaiah 6:9,10	Matthew 13:10-15
Would be rejected by His own	Psalm 69:8; Isaiah 53:3	John 1:11; 7:5
Triumphal entry into Jerusalem	Zechariah 9:9	Matthew 21:4,5
Betrayed for 30 pieces of silver	Psalm 41:9; 55:12-14; Zechariah 11:12,13	Matthew 26:14-16,21-25
Abandoned by His disciples	Zechariah 13:7	Matthew 26:31
Whipped and spat upon	Isaiah 50:6	Matthew 26:67; 27:26
Crucified between two thieves	Isaiah 53:12	Matthew 27:38; Mark 15:27,28; Luke 22:37
Would rise from the dead	Psalm 16:10	Matthew 28:2-7
Would ascend into heaven	Psalm 24:7-10	Mark 16:19; Luke 24:51

from severe persecution by the Jewish religious
leaders as well as Roman civil authorities. Many of
the letters were written to rekindle hope of Christ's
return to earth (at which time their suffering would
end as Christ established His eternal kingdom).

Vision of the future (Revelation). When it comes to
prophecies about the end of the world, this is the book
everyone is interested in. The apostle John wrote this
book while he was exiled on the island of Patmos in
the Mediterranean Sea. It was addressed to the seven
churches of Asia who were experiencing persecution
under the Romans. The book records a series of visions
John received from God dealing with how human history will end and what will happen to all people who
have ever lived. At times, these visions are confusing,
and often they're downright bizarre!

WHAT ARE THE ODDS?

Dr. Hugh Ross, a well-known astrophysicist, says that the
Bible contains approximately 2500 predictions about future events. He has determined that 2000 of the prophecies
have already been fulfilled in every detail without a single
error (500 prophecies are about events which haven't happened yet).

Science considers any probability greater than 1 in 10^{50} as
impossible. Dr. Ross has calculated that the odds of 2000
predictions coming true without error are 1 in 10^{2000}. There
is only one explanation for how so many predictions in
the Bible could come true: God.

Auditing the Old Testament Prophet Statements

A great deal of Old Testament prophecy about the end of the world pertains to what will happen to the Jews, the nation of Israel, and the city of Jerusalem. There's a very logical explanation for this emphasis, and it has to do with the *context* and the *message* of the Old Testament prophecies about the future. If you know the context and message underlying the Old Testament prophecies, you have an important key to understanding what Old testament prophets were saying about the events which will occur at the end of time.

A Covenant Context

When the Old Testament prophets spoke about the end of the world, their prophecies were given in the context of the covenant. Let us explain what we mean.

Early in the history of the human race, God made a promise (a "covenant") with Abraham. God promised several things to him:

✓ A great nation would come from the descendants of Abraham (which was pretty amazing since Abraham and his wife were both almost 100 years old at the time, and they had no children—see Genesis 12:2). The descendants of Abraham are the Jews, and the nation is now known as Israel.

✓ The descendants of Abraham would have their own homeland (see Genesis 15:7). Back then, the specific property was known as Canaan. Now it is known as Israel, including the city of Jerusalem and the land currently occupied by the Palestinians.

✓ Through a descendant of Abraham, all the nations of the world will be blessed (see Genesis 22:18). This mystery descendant was referred to as the Messiah, who would eventually come and establish a kingdom ("the messianic kingdom").

As the Old Testament prophets looked toward the end of the world, they saw it from the perspective of the Messiah coming to earth to establish His kingdom. They saw this as the fulfillment of God's covenant with Abraham.

A Message of Hope So They Could Cope

Keep in mind that most of the Old Testament prophets were writing at a time when the Jews were under terrible oppression (in many cases even being held captive in foreign countries). Their prophecies anticipated the arrival of the Messiah to restore the Jews to their homeland and establish the privileged treatment which God had promised for the descendants of Abraham. These prophecies were intended to be reassuring predictions about the end of the world which would give the Jews hope for the future. In essence, the message of the Old Testament prophets went something like this: "While things are

Two! Two! Two Prophecies in One!

Many Bible scholars believe that certain Old Testament prophecies have double coverage. They referred to an event relating to the circumstances of the prophet's own generation, and they also pointed to a future event at the end of the world. For example, the prophet Isaiah gave a prophecy about a woman and her child that related to the circumstances of King Ahaz. Centuries later, the apostle Matthew used this prophecy of Isaiah to apply to the birth of Jesus. Part of the difficulty in understanding prophecy is determining whether it was applicable to the prophet's own time, or to the end of the world, or to both.

currently bad, they aren't always going to stay that way. God is going to be faithful to the promises He made to our forefather Abraham. Hang in there! Hope is on the horizon."

So That's How It's Gonna Be

Now that you've got a grasp on the context and underlying message of the end-of-the-world predictions by the Old Testament prophets, let's look at just a few of the specific topics about which the Old Testament prophets made predictions:

Signs of the Last Days

✓ Increase of wars and rumors of wars (Joel 3:9,10).

✓ Increase in knowledge (Daniel 12:4).

Nature of the Tribulation

✓ People will hide in caves because of their fear of God (Isaiah 2:19).

✓ Sorrow of death will seize men like a woman's pains of childbirth (Isaiah 13:8).

✓ A plague will make people like walking corpses with their flesh rotting away (Zechariah 14:12).

✓ The sun, moon, and stars will darken (Joel 2:31).

✓ World events will steadily go from bad to worse (Amos 5:19).

✓ The Bible will be scarce (Amos 8:11,12).

✓ Men's blood will be poured out into the dust (Zephaniah 1:17).

✓ The earth will convulse and tremble like a drunkard (Isaiah 24:20).

✓ There will be unprecedented terror and anguish (Jeremiah 30:7).

Events Occurring with the Tribulation

✓ The Antichrist makes a seven-year peace treaty with Israel (Daniel 9:27).

✓ Jews from around the world will return to Jerusalem (Isaiah 43:5,6; Ezekiel 34:11-13).

✓ The Antichrist will desecrate the temple in Jerusalem (Daniel 9:27).

✓ A great war in Israel (Ezekiel 38:1–39:24).

✓ The battle of Armageddon will take place (Joel 3:2,9-16).

Israel's Status in the Millennium

✓ The temple will be rebuilt (Isaiah 2:2).

✓ The reign of the Messiah will be seen by the Jews (Isaiah 52:7-12).

✓ Israel will be restored by God (Isaiah 43:1-13).

✓ Jesus will rule from Jerusalem (Psalm 2:6-8).

✓ Jerusalem will become the worship center of the world (Micah 4:1).

YOU CAN KNOW THE SECRET THAT THE OLD TESTAMENT PROPHETS NEVER UNDERSTOOD

The Old Testament prophets didn't realize that there would be two separate times when the Messiah would come to earth. They expected that the "coming of the Messiah" would be one event. This misunderstanding explains their confusion as to how the Messiah could be both a suffering servant (as referred to in Isaiah 53) and a conquering leader and commander (as in Isaiah 55:4).

Jesus cleared things up. His first visit to earth was in the role as the sacrifice for our sins, so He was crucified for us. When He returns to earth in the future ("the second coming"), it will be as the reigning Lord.

Peeking at the Future from a New Testament Point of View

The end-times prophecies in the *New* Testament shift the primary focus off the Jews, the nation of Israel, and the city of Jerusalem (which were the focal points of the *Old* Testament prophets). There is a good reason for this "out with the Old, and in with the New." It has to do with Jesus Christ and what He accomplished when He was crucified.

The Context Is the Cross

When Jesus and the apostles spoke about the end of the world, their prophecies were in the context of the cross.

- ✓ The Old testament prophets had promised a Messiah who would deliver Israel from oppression by its enemies. So the Jews were expecting a Messiah who would bring them political, economic, and religious freedom.

- ✓ Christ was the Messiah who came to save the world. But His first coming was not intended to establish a political kingdom. By His death on the cross, He paid the penalty so people could be free from slavery to sin.

- ✓ Salvation through faith in Christ is available to all people. This is the fulfillment of God's promise to Abraham that the whole world would be blessed through one of his descendants (and as a Jew, Jesus was a descendant of Abraham).

✓ At some unknown moment in the future, Christ is going to return to be reunited with all people who have believed that they are saved by His death on the cross. Because He was sacrificed in our place on the cross, we have the opportunity to live with Him forever when the world as we know it comes to an end.

When the writers of the New Testament speak of the events at the end of the world, they see these things as the completion of what Christ started when He died on the cross for our sins.

A Message of Hope So They Could Cope (the Sequel)

Imagine that you are one of the 12 disciples having dinner with Jesus. You are thinking that He is about to make a public announcement that He is going to establish His earthly kingdom. To your shock, He says that He is going to be crucified the next day. You are so shocked that you don't even understand what He means when He says He will rise from the dead after three days and then go back to heaven. All you know is that your best friend in the world is soon to be out of this world. All of your dreams and aspirations for the future were tied up in this guy. How are you going to cope without Him around?

Knowing that these thoughts were haunting His disciples, Jesus reassured them with these words:

Don't be troubled. You trust God, now trust in me.
There are many rooms in my Father's home, and I am
going to prepare a place for you. If this were not so, I
would tell you plainly. When everything is ready, I
will come and get you, so that you will always be
with me where I am. And you now where I am going
and how to get there (John 14:1-3).

Whenever He spoke about the future, Jesus wanted
His disciples to be reassured that God had a master
plan. He left them with hope for the future because
the plan included living eternally with Christ Himself.

Hope and encouragement were also the underlying
message of the end-times prophecies given by the
writers of the epistles. For instance, the new believers
in the city of Thessalonica were under the impression
that Christ's second coming was going to happen immediately. When some of them died before the
second coming, the others were confused and depressed. Paul, therefore, wrote a letter to that church
explaining that all of the dead believers would be
resurrected with new bodies at the return of Christ.
He didn't want them to be sorrowful if Christ's return was delayed. Instead, he wanted them to be excited about the prospect of being reunited with their
deceased loved ones at some time in the future:

Then, together with them, we who are still alive and
remain on the earth will be caught up in the clouds to
meet the Lord in the air and remain with him forever.
So comfort and encourage each other with these
words (1 Thessalonians 4:17,18).

As with the end-times prophecies from the Old Testament, the message behind the prophecies in the New Testament is one of hope.

Look at the View from Here

Because you now know the context and underlying message of the New Testament prophecies, you will be better able to make sense of the specific predictions given by Jesus and the apostles. Let's take a look at a few of their statements.

Signs of the Last Days (as Told by Jesus)

- ✓ There will be wars and rumors of wars (Matthew 24:6).

- ✓ There will be conflict between the nations (Matthew 24:7).

- ✓ There will be famines and earthquakes (Matthew 24:7).

- ✓ Christians will be martyred (Matthew 24:9).

- ✓ There will be an increase in wickedness (Matthew 24:12).

Signs of the Last Days (as Predicted by Paul)

- ✓ Christians will be snatched off the face of the earth into the sky (1 Thessalonians 4:17).

- ✓ Bodies of dead Christians will be pulled out of the graves (1 Thessalonians 4:16).

Nature of the Tribulation (as Predicted by John)

✓ There will be famines and plagues (Revelation 6:8).

✓ Christians will be martyred (Revelation 6:9).

✓ Earthquakes and natural calamities will kill up to half the world's population (Revelation 6:12; 8:7; 11:19).

Events Occurring with the Tribulation (as Predicted by John)

✓ A devious world leader will seek world domination (Revelation 6:2).

✓ This world leader will institute a false religion (Revelation 13:11-15).

✓ There will be a move toward a global economy, and anyone who refuses allegiance to the world leader cannot participate in commerce (Revelation 13:16-18).

For extra credit, go back to page 111 and see how the end-times prophecies of the Old Testament coincide with the end-of-the-world predictions in the New Testament.

Strained Eyesight . . . Blurred Vision . . . or Just Poor Lighting?

Are you looking at our Bible map of prophecy and still having a hard time seeing how it lays out? Are you worried that you might just have poor eyesight when it comes to seeing things of the future? Are you frustrated that your "end of the world" vision seems impaired because of your lack of understanding? Well, don't despair. And cancel that appointment for your eyeball rotation and lobotomy lube job.

God doesn't expect you to see a completed and detailed picture of all that will happen at the end of the world. In fact, He doesn't want you to know everything. Some things He intends to keep hidden from our understanding.

> *No one knows the day or the hour when these things will happen, not even the angels in heaven or the Son himself. Only the Father knows* (Matthew 24:36).

If God had wanted all of this to be plain and simple for us, He could have made it that way. Instead, He intentionally chose to obscure many of the details about the end of the world. So it's not that you have poor end-times eyesight; it's just that God has purposefully kept the lighting dim. We can see the large shapes of what is on the horizon, but we still can't make out the details. Here is how the apostle Paul explained it:

> *Now we see things imperfectly as in a poor mirror, but then we will see everything with perfect clarity. All that I know now is partial and incomplete, but then I will know everything completely, just as God knows me now* (1 Corinthians 13:12).

So we don't need to be frustrated if we feel a little disoriented in our study of the end times. God wants us to know enough to be confident that He has a plan for us, and to place our hope for the future in His plan.

"What's That Again?"

1. Prophecies about the end times appear throughout the Bible. They are not arranged in any kind of sequential order.

2. In the Old Testament, most of the end-times prophecies are found in the books of the major and minor prophets. In the New Testament, Jesus and the writers of the epistles refer to some of the events which will happen in the future, but Revelation is essentially an entire book about the events at the end of time.

3. When the Old Testament prophets spoke about the end of the world, their prophecies were in the context of the covenant.

4. Prophecies about the end of the world from the New Testament were in the context of the cross.

5. In both the Old and New Testaments, the prophecies about the end of the world carry a message of hope that God will be faithful to His promises.

6. Don't expect to understand all of this now. God didn't intend for us to know everything in this lifetime.

Dig Deeper

Most books about the end times include sections about specific Bible prophecies. Here are several books which can help you understand the "big picture" of prophecy.

The Prophecy Study Bible. This is the entire Bible, and the study notes explain the prophecies from Genesis through Revelation in relation to the end times. The general editor, John C. Hagee, is a prominent scholar on the topic of the end of the world.

The Prophecy Knowledge Handbook by Dr. John F. Walvoord is a collection of all the prophecies of the Bible. Arranged in the sequence of the books of the Bible, each passage of prophetical significance is explained.

The Encyclopedia of Biblical Prophecy by J. Barton Payne is similar in format to Dr. Walvoord's book. It provides an explanation of the meaning of all the prophecy verses in the Bible.

If you think that tackling all the Bible verses at once is a little too intimidating, you might want to start on a smaller scale. Try *God's Blueprint for Bible Prophecy* by a really great Bible teacher, Kay Arthur. This book is designed to be a 13-week Bible study of the Old Testament Book of Daniel.

We also heartily recommend *Fast Facts on Bible Prophecy* by Thomas Ice and Timothy Demy. This book is arranged like an expanded glossary—the subjects are arranged alphabetically. You won't need a lot of background in Bible prophecy to understand the concise explanations in this book.

Moving On . . .

We hope we have given you a little better understanding about how the end-times prophecies of the Bible fit together. To finish the analogy we started with, we hope you now know how to read the Bible map. But knowing where to look in the Bible and understanding the background and context of the prophecies is just the first step. These are matters of *location* and *relation*—about these matters there is almost universal agreement. Where the big difference of opinion exists (and that is putting it mildly) is the area of *interpretation*.

Don't think for even a brief moment that all of the experts agree on a biblical scenario for the end of the world. They don't agree. They strongly disagree. They would probably even come to blows over their opinions if it wasn't for the fact that most of them are bookworm types who don't know how to clench a fist.

If even the experts can't agree, how can you be expected to make sense out of the obscure prophetic passages of the Bible? Well, you've got one thing that the experts don't have: You've got Bruce and Stan (actually, that's two things). Don't get us wrong. We aren't saying that we're smarter than the experts. We're just saying that we understand your confusion and we'll help you make sense of what all the arguing is about.

Chapter 5

If It's God's Word, Why Is Everyone Arguing About It?

Prophecy is not so difficult that we can't understand it, or else God would not have put it into Scripture.

—*Tim LaHaye*

Just because we don't understand something doesn't mean that we don't believe it is valuable and true. For example, to this day, men have not figured out women, yet we still know they are valuable and true (our wives told us to say that).

The same principle applies to Bible prophecy. Sure, it can be complicated and confusing. But that doesn't mean it isn't valuable and true, and it doesn't mean you shouldn't go to the trouble of trying to understand it. Prophecy is valuable precisely because it is true 100 percent of the time. The reason we can say that is because all prophecy comes from God (2 Peter 1:20), and everything God says is true (otherwise He wouldn't be God).

At the same time, there are things about prophecy we will never understand, just as there are things about God (and women) that we will never understand. So don't be discouraged, but rather be encouraged as you study God's Word, asking Him to open your heart and mind to the truth.

Bruce & Stan

Chapter 5

If It's God's Word, Why Is Everyone Arguing About It?

What's Ahead

➤ Why so much disagreement?
➤ The most important things
➤ The rest is important, but not essential
➤ What's the best way to study Bible prophecy?
➤ So how do you interpret prophecy?
➤ So what's the difference?

A couple of years ago we each took our families on a European vacation (Bruce went to Paris, and Stan went to Vienna). We highly recommend this if you are 1) interested in expanding your cultural horizons or 2) want to experience new levels of frustration.

Finding your way around in a large European city is no easy assignment. It may look organized and picturesque from the air, but once you land and start driving around, you quickly discover how confusing the streets are. Even when you get out your English map, you find that the street names are still in a foreign language, and none of the streets flow in an orderly direction.

"Why Do We Argue?"

There has been disagreement over God's plan for the future and the end of the world since Jesus left the earth and returned to heaven nearly 2000 years ago. We agree on the fact that Christ is going to return to earth a second time, but we disagree on the chronology and meaning of end-times events. Here are some of the reasons why:

✓ The Bible is pretty vague on some of the future stuff.

✓ Whenever anyone studies prophecy, that person comes with his or her own agenda.

✓ People interpret the Bible differently.

✓ Many base their viewpoint on ever-changing world events.

✓ Some people are more naturally optimistic or pessimistic than others.

Even the landmarks don't always help. When you're flying overhead, you're confident that you will be able to spot them once you're on the ground. But once in the city, you easily lose your sense of orientation. All you can see is the street in front of you.

Why So Much Disagreement?

Trying to figure out the meaning of a specific Bible prophecy is a lot like being in the middle of a foreign city. Even though you have the big picture in mind—you know the final destination—you lose your perspective and can end up frustrated. No wonder there's so much disagreement. We all have the same map (the Bible). We use the same words. We can read them and (sometimes!) pronounce them properly. But we often can't agree on what they mean.

We're going to dig into the things we agree on—as well as some of the things we don't—a little later in the chapter. Before we do that, we think it is important to give you a little historical perspective on how Christians through the centuries have viewed the end times (we're grateful for the information provided by Richard Kyle in his excellent book *The Last Days Are Here Again*):

✓ Most Christians in the **first century** believed that the world was going to end in their lifetime. As the church became established and persecution decreased, the thinking shifted to a future kingdom of God on earth (known as the millennium).

✓ In the **second century**, Iranaeus, the bishop of Lyons, taught that there would be a literal Antichrist who would rule the earth for three and a half years, followed by the return of Christ and a literal millennium on earth that would resemble the perfect conditions in the

Garden of Eden. After that would come eternity. His view later became known as *premillennialism*.

✓ Origen, a theologian in the **third century**, disagreed with the idea that the millennium would be a 1000-year paradise on earth. Instead of interpreting the Scriptures literally in these matters of prophecy, he chose to take an allegorical approach (we'll get into the comparison between literal and allegorical later in this chapter).

✓ In the **fourth century**, St. Augustine, the bishop of Hippo, taught that Christ had established the millennium at His first coming. He said, "The church now on earth is both the kingdom of Christ and the kingdom of heaven." His view later became known as *amillennialism*.

✓ During the **Middle Ages** (around 1100 to 1500) people became preoccupied with the end times. The rise of Islam in the Middle East, the Black Plague in Europe, and the changing political climate caused many to think that the Antichrist was about to emerge and the end of the world would arrive soon.

✓ In the **sixteenth century** the great Reformer Martin Luther believed he was living in the last days. Like most of the Reformers, he believed that the millennium either had already happened, or that it was spiritual in nature.

✓ In the **seventeenth century** the English Puritans (the same ones who came to America in search of religious freedom in 1620) went back to the view that there would be a future literal millennium.

✓ Jonathan Edwards, the famous **eighteenth century** American preacher, believed and taught that the various religious revivals, such as the Great Awakening in the 1740s, would bring about the millennium, after which Christ would return. This view was known as *postmillennialism.*

✓ In the **nineteenth century**, an Irishman by the name of John Darby came up with the idea of *dispensationalism,* which teaches that God has dealt with humankind through a series of ages or "dispensations." Since the first coming of Jesus, we have been living in the "Church Age," which will be followed by the end times. Kyle writes that "dispensationalism far exceeds other belief systems in promoting end-time thinking" because the dispensationalist believes that the second coming of Christ can happen any time.

✓ In the **twentieth century**, dispensationalism was further popularized by two books: *The Scofield Reference Bible,* first published in 1909, and *The Late Great Planet Earth,* written by Hal Lindsey and published in 1970. In between the publication of these two highly popular books, two world wars and the rise of nuclear weapons fueled the belief that we are in the end times and that Christ could return at any moment.

Before we get into some of the more popular viewpoints about the end of the world, we want to make
two very important statements about this whole topic.
Read these carefully. As far as we're concerned, these
two statements may be the most important things you
read in this whole book. Are you ready? Here they are:

✓ It's okay to disagree over Bible prophecy.

✓ Never lose sight of your destination.

Here's what we mean. . .

It's Okay to Disagree over Bible Prophecy

Good people on all sides of these issues have disagreed for 2000 years. This book is certainly not going
to cause everyone to agree, and that's okay. When we
say "good" people, we mean people who believe in
the inspiration and authority of Scripture. We mean
people who believe in and long for the return of
Christ. Throughout your life, you're going to meet fine
Christian people who disagree with you on many of
these issues. Love them. Learn from them. Have fun
disagreeing with them on the timing of Christ's return
and the events surrounding it. But don't become so
caught up in the disagreements that you lose the most
important thing: a focus on what truly does matter.

Never Lose Sight of Your Destination

There's an old saying: "Life's a journey—enjoy the
ride." More than likely you've also heard that the
process is more important than the end result. That

may be true in some cases, but when it comes to the Christian life, the destination is what counts. Yes, the process is important (it's called *life*), but without the final reward—the ultimate destination of being with God for all eternity—this little span of time each of us spends on earth wouldn't be worth a whole lot, especially when you measure our days against eternity.

Here's what the psalmist David wrote:

> *Our days on earth are like grass; like wildflowers, we bloom and die. The wind blows, and we are gone—as though we had never been here* (Psalm 103:15,16).

The apostle Paul put it this way:

> *Forgetting the past and looking forward to what lies ahead, I strain to reach the end of the race and receive the prize for which God, through Christ Jesus, is calling us up to heaven* (Philippians 3:13,14).

You see, the Christian life really boils down to one thing: Jesus Christ. Without Christ, there is no Christianity. Without Christ, there is no hope of salvation. Without Christ, there is no hope of heaven.

You can't very well say, "Even if there really were no heaven, being a Christian would still be worth it, because at least I would be a better person." Wrong thinking! If there's no heaven, there's no salvation. We're not just saved *from* something (eternal death). We are saved *to* something (eternal life).

C. S. Lewis said, "If Christianity is untrue, then no honest man will want to believe it, however helpful it might be; if it is true, every honest man will want to believe it, even if it gives him no help at all."

The Most Important Things

What then, is it critical for us to agree on? We believe there are a handful of "the most important things," and they all have to do with Jesus Christ:

✓ Everything came into existence through Jesus Christ.

> *Christ is the one through whom God created everything in heaven and earth. He made the things we can see and the things we can't see— kings, kingdoms, rulers, and authorities. Every-thing has been created through him and for him. He existed before everything else began, and he holds all creation together* (Colossians 1:16,17).

✓ When humanity rebelled against God, Jesus Christ came to earth to save us from God's judgment.

> *But God showed his great love for us by sending Christ to die for us while we were still sinners. And since we have been made right in God's sight by the blood of Christ, he will certainly save us from God's judgment* (Romans 5:8,9).

✔ Jesus Christ is the only way to God.

> *Jesus told him, "I am the way, the truth, and the life. No one can come to the Father except through me"* (John 14:6).

✔ At some future time, God's plan to bring human history to a close will center on Christ.

> *God's secret plan has now been revealed to us; it is a plan centered on Christ, designed long ago according to his good pleasure. And this is his plan: At the right time he will bring everything together under the authority of Christ—everything in heaven and on earth* (Ephesians 1:9,10).

Gilbert Bilezikian writes,

> In summary, in Christ all things were made, in him all things were reclaimed, and in him all things will be fulfilled. He is the Alpha and the Omega, the beginning and the end (Revelation 21:6; 22:13). History finds meaning in him alone. Since he will bring history to its final consummation, the doctrine of the end times necessarily revolves around his Second Coming.

The Rest Is Important, But Not Essential

Okay, here's where it gets a little tricky. Here we are, about a third of the way through this book, and we're about to tell you that everything we've said so far has been important (or essential) and everything from now on will be nonessential. Well, technically that's true, if by "nonessential" we mean "nonessential to your faith and your future" (and we do).

In other words, as far as your eternal salvation is concerned, the following stuff really doesn't matter:

- ✓ The timing of the tribulation
- ✓ Whether or not Christians will go through the tribulation
- ✓ Whether or not there will be a literal 1000-year reign of Christ on earth
- ✓ How you interpret the complicated images and symbols in the book of Revelation

If any of these things (and more) really did make a difference in the condition of our eternal souls, then God would have said so in His Word. But He didn't. What the Bible does say is that our salvation and eternal future with God rest on His grace and our faith in Jesus Christ. Nothing more, nothing less.

God saved you by his special favor when you believed. And you can't take credit for this; it is a gift from God. Salvation is not a reward for the good things we have done, so none of us can boast about it. For we are God's masterpiece. He has created us anew in Christ Jesus, so that we can do the good things he planned for us long ago (Ephesians 2:8-10).

Fulfilled Versus Unfulfilled Prophecy

It's important to make a distinction between *fulfilled* prophecy and *unfulfilled* prophecy. Two-thirds of all Bible prophecies have already been fulfilled, many of them concerning the person and work of Jesus

> ### 👆 GLAD YOU ASKED *"So Why Study Prophecy?"*
>
> Or more correctly, "Why study *unfulfilled* prophecy?" We can think of several benefits both for the non-Christian and the Christian. *If you are not a Christian*, studying prophecy will give you a greater understanding of *how* God is going to deal with the human race and the world we live in, even if you can't determine *when* these things will happen. As you study prophecy, you will learn that someday (a day no one knows) God will bring all human history to a conclusion.
>
> *If you are a Christian*, then the study of prophecy will give you a greater understanding of God's plan and purpose. Although you will never understand everything, you will be able to answer basic questions of those who are concerned about the future. If your hope is tied to a future with God in Christ Jesus, then you should be able to explain the reason for that hope.
>
> *And if you are asked about your Christian hope, always be ready to explain it* (1 Peter 3:15).

Christ. *Fulfilled* prophecy is extremely important because it demonstrates the tremendous credibility of the Bible and strengthens our faith (see chapter 4).

Unfulfilled prophecy, which concerns events after the first coming of Jesus to earth (and includes God's plan for the end of the world), is also important. But it doesn't necessarily strengthen our faith. On the contrary, it is our faith in God and His plan that gives us confidence that these things are going to happen. Although we can't see what's going to happen, we believe that these things will occur, just as predicted. Here again is that wonderful verse from Hebrews:

What is faith? It is the confident assurance that what we hope for is going to happen. It is the evidence of things we cannot yet see (Hebrews 11:1).

What's the Best Way to Study Bible Prophecy?

The way you study and understand Bible prophecy will be determined by how you *interpret* the Bible. We're going to talk about the two most prominent methods of biblical interpretation. They are:

- ✔ The *literal* or *normal* method
- ✔ The *spiritualizing* or *allegorizing* method

The Literal or Normal Method

If you interpret the Bible literally, you interpret it *as it is*. The meaning of Scripture is determined by the *language* of the original languages (Hebrew or Greek) and the *historical context*. Since God chose to use language to convey His message (as opposed to symbols), we should take that language literally. When it comes to interpreting prophecy, the literalists like to

Then and There Versus Here and Now

According to Gordon Fee and Douglas Stuart, a student of the Bible should approach the task of interpretation on two levels:

1. Try to understand what the passage meant to the original audience, or the people who were around when a particular Bible book was first written (for example, Paul's letter to the Romans was written to the first century church in Rome). This is the *then and there* part of biblical interpretation.

2. Try to understand what that same passage means to us today. This is the *here and now* part of biblical interpretation.

When it comes to Bible prophecy, you have to do a little of both. You should do your best to discover the "original, intended meaning" as well as the "contemporary relevance of ancient texts."

point out that all fulfilled prophecy was fulfilled literally. Why should we think unfulfilled prophecy will come true in any other way?

The Spiritualizing or Allegorizing Method

Those who use the allegorical method believe it is impossible to interpret all of Scripture literally. This doesn't mean they never interpret Scripture literally.

Allegories and Parables

BRUCE & STAN SAY

When you read the Bible, you will discover many of the same classic literary tools used by all good writers. Writers use *allegory* when they are telling a story to explain an idea or get across a moral lesson. The *parables* of Jesus were allegorical in nature. For example, when Jesus said the kingdom of God was "like a tiny mustard seed planted in a garden" (Luke 13:18), He didn't mean that we would have to shrink down to the size of the characters in *Honey, I Shrunk the Kids* in order to enter the kingdom. He was using something we know about (the mustard seed) to explain something we have no idea about (the kingdom of God— you'll have to read the parable to get the lesson).

Even those who take the Bible literally allow room for allegory, in the same way that those who interpret the Bible allegorically still read the Bible literally as well. Some, however, apply the allegorical method in very broad ways. For example, it's possible (although we don't recommend it) to say that the entire Creation account in Genesis 1–2 is allegorical—in other words, a made-up story to explain how our world came to be. The problem is, once you do that, you might just as well say that God is an allegory. Our rule of thumb is this: If the allegory or parable takes away from the literal truth about God or the literal Person and work of Jesus Christ, then it has gone too far. *An allegory should never contradict the literal truth about God.*

They just contend that you can't do it 100 percent of the time. The Bible contains many different literary forms—such as poetry and prophecy—and some of these forms contain symbols and figures of speech which must be approached in a different manner. Though there are a few scholars who use this method with all of Scripture, most would agree with St. Augustine, who taught that allegorical interpretation primarily applies to unfulfilled prophecy.

So How Do You Interpret Prophecy?

**Chapter
8**

Before we get to the future details in Part III, we want to give you the three main views about God's plan for the future. Most Bible scholars agree that these views center on the millennial kingdom, which we will be talking about in chapter 8.

Premillennialism

This view, which is based on the *literal* view of Scripture, holds that Christ will return before (that's where the *pre* comes from) the millennium, which will be a literal 1000-year reign of Christ on earth. He

---

A SHORT DEFINITION OF THE MILLENNIUM

The word *millennium* actually never appears in the Bible. It comes from the Latin words *mille*, meaning "thousand," and *annus*, meaning "year." You'll find the phrase "thousand years" six times in Revelation 20.

The Imminent Return of Christ

If you hold to the pre-tribulational rapture view, then you believe that Christ could come at any time. There are no other prophecies that need to be fulfilled before Jesus returns for those who believe or have believed in Him. This is what is referred to as the *imminent* return of Christ.

will rule from His throne in Jerusalem, and Satan will be bound in the "abyss" for the entire time. The final judgment will come at the conclusion of the millennium, followed by eternity.

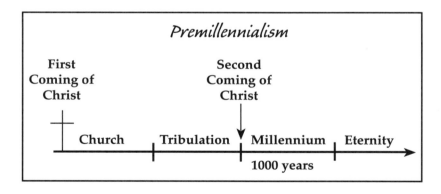

Within the premillennial view, there is disagreement regarding the tribulation (which we'll talk about in chapter 7) and the church, which is composed of all believers (except for the believers who have died and are *de*composed). Here are the views:

Chapter 7

Chapter 6

The church will be raptured before the tribulation begins. Some premillennialists have concluded that all believers, dead and alive, will be caught up in the air (or *raptured*) to be with the Lord (see chapter 6) *before* the seven-year tribulation begins. Then, after the tribulation, Christ will return to earth (in what is known as the second coming) to defeat Satan and his armies and establish the millennium. This is the premillennial *pre-tribulational* view.

The church will go through the tribulation. Some premillennialists have concluded that the church will remain on earth through the future seven-year tribulation. In this view, the rapture and the second coming happen simultaneously, after which the millennium begins. This is the premillennial *post-tribulational* view.

The church will go through the first half of the tribulation. As you will see in chapter 7, the seven-year tribulation can be divided into two parts. The first half will be relatively peaceful—perhaps more peaceful than it is now—but in the second half things will get really nasty. There is a view among some premillennialists that the church will be around for the first half of the tribulation, but will miss the second half due to the rapture. This is the premillennial *mid-tribulational* view (how did you guess?).

Amillennialism

Amillennialism basically says that there will be no future, literal 1000-year reign of Christ on earth (*a* means "no"). Generally, amillennialists don't interpret the Bible literally when it comes to unfulfilled

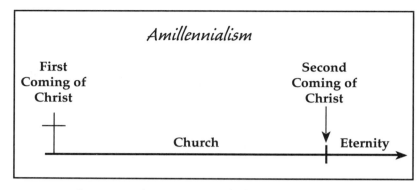

prophecy, preferring a *symbolic* or *spiritual* interpretation. There will be no literal 1000-year millennium squeezed in between Christ's return and the final judgment. In fact, we are currently living in a millennial state on earth in a spiritual kingdom—God's kingdom. This is what Jesus meant when He said, "Make the Kingdom of God your primary concern" (Matthew 6:33).

At the same time, this world is bound by Satan's kingdom. God's kingdom and Satan's kingdom co-exist now, and will continue that way until the second coming of Christ. When Christ returns, there will be a general resurrection, followed by a general judgment, followed by eternity.

Postmillennialism

Those who hold this view believe that the church is in the process of building the kingdom of God right now by being a positive influence (salt and light) in society. The term *postmillennialism* simply means that

Christ will return *after* such a kingdom has been established. Postmillennialists do not take the "thousand years" of Revelation 20 literally. According to Lightner, the primary part of this belief system is "its belief in the final triumph of good over evil before Christ returns." When Christ does return, this age will end and eternity will begin.

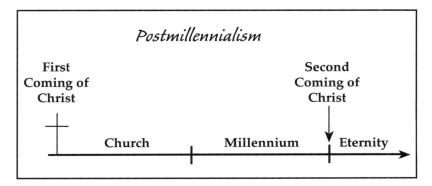

So What's the Difference?

After reading about the different viewpoints on the end of the world, you will probably reach one of three conclusions.

What's the Big Deal?

By now *you're bored*. All of this speculation about the end times is so picky. You think all of this talk about the end of the world is counterproductive, if not outright boring. So you let out a big yawn and decide to concentrate on the here and now rather than the then and there. After all, nobody ever accomplished anything by standing around looking up. You've got to put your nose to the grindstone and help people in need. What we need to do is change things *now* so that this world will become a better place for the future. It might be a while before Jesus returns, so let's not waste our effort on empty speculation.

What's the Difference?

Instead, you may identify with those people we've heard say, *"Pre, mid, post...*what's the difference? I'm a *pan*-millennialist—it's all going to *pan* out in the end." You are interested in the end of the world and the Lord's return, but you don't want to get bogged down in the details. Consequently, *you shrug your shoulders* and go on living as if it doesn't really matter. You're busy with your family, your work, your church, and your recreation. Who has time to worry about the Lord's return?

I've Got to Know More

Or, you may be frustrated with us because we're moving too slow. You can't wait to get to the nitty-gritty details because you're looking for that one big sign that will signal the end. *Your eyes are focused on the end*, scanning the daily headlines looking for signs of famines, earthquakes, and wars. You're convinced there's a supercomputer somewhere in Europe code-named "the Beast." You've read every prophecy book ever written (including this one, thank you very much), and you've even had Hal Lindsey over for dinner.

Prophecy Is No Good Unless . . .

As we have already stated in this book, Bible prophecy *is* incredibly important. But it can be completely useless to you in your life unless...

It encourages you to watch and pray. If you're a yawner and you get bored with all the end-times clatter, this message is for you. Be alert, be wise, be in prayer. *Jesus is going to return.* Pay special attention to the story Jesus told to illustrate how He wants us to act until He returns:

> *The coming of the Son of Man can be compared with that of a man who left home to go on a trip. He gave each of his employees instructions about the work they were to do, and he told the gatekeeper to watch for his return. So keep a sharp lookout! For you do not know when the homeowner will return—at evening, midnight, early dawn, or late daybreak. Don't let him find you sleeping when he arrives without warning. What I say to you I say to everyone: Watch for his return!* (Mark 13:34-37).

It encourages you to please God. If you have a tendency to shrug your shoulders and get caught up in earthly concerns, remember that *Jesus is going to judge our deeds.* Go about your life, but keep in mind that only what you do for Christ and His kingdom will last into eternity. Make it your goal to do everything in a way that pleases God.

> *So think clearly and exercise self-control. Look forward to the special blessings that will come to you at the return of Christ. . . . And remember that the heavenly Father to whom you pray has no favorites when he judges. He will judge or reward you according to what you do. So you must live in reverent fear of him during your time as foreigners here on earth* (1 Peter 1:13,17).

It encourages you to encourage others. If your eyes are focused on the end to the extent that you've forgotten about the present, you need to consider those around you. Don't isolate yourself behind a wall of speculation. Rather, follow the wise advice of Scripture:

> *Think of ways to encourage one another to outbursts of love and good deeds. And let us not neglect our meeting together, as some people do, but encourage and warn each other, especially now that the day of his coming back again is drawing near* (Hebrews 10:24,25).

It encourages you to tell others about Jesus. The last instruction Jesus gave to His disciples was to tell others about Him. The clearest record of His words, commonly known as the Great Commission, is found in the Gospel of Mark:

> *Go into all the world and preach the Good News to everyone, everywhere* (Mark 16:15).

This very clear command is not a suggestion. Everyone who knows Jesus personally has a responsibility before God to share the "Good News" with those who have not accepted Him as God's provision for eternal life (that's what the Good News really is).

"What's That Again?"

1. There has been disagreement over God's plan for the future ever since Jesus left the earth.

2. It's okay to disagree over Bible prophecy, as long as we never lose sight of our eternal destination.

3. God's plan has always centered on Jesus Christ, including His plan for the future. The main event of the end times is His second coming.

4. Fulfilled prophecy demonstrates the credibility of the Bible. It is our faith in God and His plan that gives us confidence in prophecy as yet unfulfilled.

5. There are different ways to interpret Bible prophecy, and they are based upon the way you interpret the Bible.

6. The three main views of God's plan for the future center on the millennial kingdom.

7. Prophecy is no good unless it encourages us to watch and pray, please God, and encourage one another.

Dig Deeper

 The following books on the differing views of prophecy can get a little complicated. But if you're ready to expand your mind, dig in:

The Coming Millennial Kingdom by Donald Campbell and Jeffrey Townsend. Campbell and Townsend are proponents of dispensationalism and premillennialism. In this book they have collected articles from 14 scholars who join together to provide a thorough presentation of the premillennial interpretation.

The Last Days According to Jesus by R. C. Sproul. Our favorite theologian, unlike us, favors the amillennial view of prophecy. In Dr. Sproul's first book about the end times, he focuses on what Jesus said about the end times.

How to Read the Bible for All Its Worth by Gordon Fee and Douglas Stuart. We've recommended this book before because we like it. It contains excellent guidance on how to interpret the Bible.

The Last Days Are Here Again by Richard Kyle. This is the book to read for a complete history of end-times fever—a condition that's been with us for at least 2000 years.

Lectures in Theology by Henry Thiessen. This classic book of systematic theology holds to the premillennial view of the end of the world.

Systematic Theology by L. Berkhof. This book of systematic theology takes the classic Reformed amillennial position on the end of the world.

Moving On . . .

You have been very patient as we have built the foundation of this book before getting to the structure itself. In Part III we're going to construct an end-times scenario, beginning with the rapture and ending with heaven.

We're pretty confident that the rapture is going to trigger the events leading to the end of the world, while heaven will complete them. As for the stuff in between, we're pretty sure they're going to happen, but we want to remind you that the *order* of these events isn't written in stone. We're even willing to concede that one or two of the things we're going to talk about may not happen at all, at least not in the way we've described them.

We aren't apologizing for this, because even the apostle Paul—the greatest theologian ever—wrote, "Now we see things imperfectly as in a poor mirror" (1 Corinthians 13:12). *No kidding!* Paul also wrote, "All I know now is partial and incomplete." *Amen to that, brother!* We *don't* know everything. But you know what? Someday we will! Someday "we will see everything with perfect clarity." Someday we will "know everything completely," just as God knows us completely now.

That should give you a great deal of comfort and confidence as you read about the amazing things coming at the end of the world.

PART III:

THE BAD NEWS . . . AND THE GOOD NEWS

Look! Up in the sky! It's a bird . . . it's a plane . . . no, it's a Christian.

We want to welcome all of you who skipped the first 151 pages and are starting to read the book at this chapter. We don't blame you, and our feelings aren't hurt (although we think you have missed some pretty good stuff that you'll want to read later). We recognize that the chapters in Part III cover the subjects that you are *really* interested in, and you just can't wait to get to them.

Well, we can't wait to tell you about them. Some of the events at the end of the world will be strange and bizarre, others will be fantastically wonderful, still others will be utterly horrible. Some of them will be terrible and marvelous at the same time, depending upon your relationship with God. A good example of what we mean is explained in this next chapter. For those who get sucked up by the rapture, their problems are over; but it won't be a pretty picture for the folks who get left behind.

Get ready to read about the rapture ride—it's out of this world!

Bruce & Stan

Chapter 6

The Rapture: Now You See Me, Now You Don't

What's Ahead

➤ The "I'll be back" guarantee
➤ The great vanishing act
➤ What to know about those who go
➤ Sad to say, some will stay
➤ Three views of when
➤ So what does all this mean to you?

*D*id you ever have the experience of being "left behind"? Maybe you were on a family car trip as a kid and your parents drove off, forgetting you were still in the gas station restroom. Maybe you were at Disneyworld with your teenagers and they ditched you at the jungle cruise ride. Or maybe you were rushing to catch a cruise ship and got to the pier just as the ship was leaving the dock. Being left behind is never fun, but you get over it.

One of the events at the end of world will leave a lot of people behind . . . but they will never get over it. This event, called "the rapture," will happen suddenly and without warning. In just seconds, millions of people will disappear off the face of the earth, vanishing into the sky. Even dead bodies will be yanked from their graves and shot upward. Back on earth, for those left behind, there will be a lot of chaos, confusion, and scrambling to find a Bible—any Bible—as people look for explanations ("Grandma was always reading a Bible. Let's find hers. Hey! Where *is* Grandma?").

The "I'll Be Back" Guarantee

The night before His crucifixion, Jesus was having dinner with His disciples (the "last supper"). They were clueless as to what was going to happen. In fact, they thought He was about to lead a political revolt and overthrow the Jewish religious leaders and the Roman military. Jesus shocked them with the news

"THE RAPTURE"

The "rapture" is the event when all Christians, living and dead, will be raised up into the sky to meet Jesus and then remain with Him forever. The word *rapture* is not in the Bible, but comes from the Latin word *rapio*, which means "caught up." This is a Latin translation of the Greek expression used by the apostle Paul when he explained the rapture:

Then, together with them [the Christians who have died], we who are still alive and remain on the earth will be caught up in the clouds to meet the Lord in the air and remain with him forever (1 Thessalonians 4:17).

that He was going to die, that He would rise from the grave after three days, and that He would return to heaven. But Jesus wanted them to know that He was not abandoning them on this hostile planet. He promised to come back and get them:

Don't be troubled. You trust God, now trust in me. There are many rooms in my Father's home, and I am going to prepare a place for you. If this were not so, I would tell you plainly. **When everything is ready, I will come and get you,** *so that you will always be with me where I am* (John 14:1-3).

Notice the three-part promise which Christ made:

1. He will come back from heaven . . .
2. For the purpose of retrieving His followers . . .
3. So that they can spend eternity with Him!

All three elements of that promise will be fulfilled when the rapture occurs.

The Great Vanishing Act

It might happen tomorrow, or maybe next month or next year. Or it might happen a few decades from now. No one knows *when* it will happen, but it *will* happen. And it might go something like this:

✓ *A shout and a trumpet blast.* The gray of the early morning dawn is

---

The End of the World According to Hollywood

Waterworld suggests that the world is going to come to a cataclysmic end as the result of global warming. After viewing this tiresome movie, however, most people have the mental picture of a bomb.

shattered by a brilliant light that penetrates the drapes and curtains of every home. There is a thunderous shout—in an unknown language—like the sound of a nuclear explosion whose sonic waves actually knock people to the ground. The deafening shout is followed by a piercing, blaring sound that is literally painful.

✓ *A global event.* This is not an isolated incident. It happens simultaneously around the globe. Every living person on planet Earth is startled to attention. Fear petrifies them in place.

✓ *The dead come back to life.* The first movement comes from cemeteries around the world. The graves of people buried during the last 2000 years are breaking open, causing a putrid stench to fill the air. Bodies actually rise from the ground, but these are not rotting corpses. These are healthy, robust human beings that are *alive.* They seem to hover above the ground momentarily, even greeting each other, before being pulled upward into the sky.

✓ *Physical transformation.* An instant later, millions of people from all parts of the earth feel a tingling sensation pulsating throughout their bodies. They are all suddenly energized. Those with physical deformities are healed. The blind suddenly see. Wrinkles disappear on the elderly as their youth is restored. As these people marvel at their physical transformation, they are lifted skyward. Those in buildings pass right through the ceilings and roof without pain or damage. It seems that their flesh and bones can dematerialize, defying all known laws of physics and biology. As they travel heavenward, some of them see and greet those who have risen from their graves. There is a mystical reunion of sorts, and then suddenly, they all vanish from sight.

✓ *Mass catastrophe.* Calamities around the world follow in the moments that pass. Jumbo jets plummet to earth, as they no longer have a pilot at the controls. Driverless buses, trains, subways, and cars cause unimaginable disaster. Classrooms are suddenly without teachers. Riots break out in the prisons as guards are suddenly absent from their stations. Doctors and nurses seem to abandon their patients in the middle of surgical operations, or patients vanish from the operating table. Children disappear from their beds. People run through the streets looking for missing family members who were there just moments ago. Panic grips every household, city, and country.

✓ *Questions without answers.* Members of the news media quickly look for answers and explanations. Ted Turner assigns his CNN reporters to interview politicians, scholars, and scientists. Someone makes a vague reference to an ancient myth that predicted a mysterious departure of Christians from the earth. When several reporters are dispatched to get a comment from

Billy Graham, he can't be located. Several other "religious dignitaries" are available, and they discount the rapture theory as being a biblical allegory and not an actual event.

✓ *Economic chaos.* In the days that follow, the global economies falter. Bankers ponder how to collect on the unpaid loans of the millions who have disappeared. Billions of dollars are frozen in brokerage trading accounts until the problem can be solved.

✓ *Anything but the truth.* As order is restored over the next weeks, the world leaders report that their experts determined the cause of the cataclysmic event: It was a UFO invasion. Many of the earth's citizens have been abducted by aliens.

The End of the World According to Hollywood

Deep Impact. With a giant asteroid on a collision course with earth, the lucky winners of the ultimate lottery proceed to the underground shelter where the government has been secretly stockpiling granola bars. (The rest of the world prepares to be toast.)

If you think we are making all of this up . . . if you think this is pure fiction . . . keep reading, because such a scenario is consistent with the Bible's description of the rapture.

What To Know About Those Who Go

The concept of the rapture was not revealed by God to the Old Testament prophets. It was an event first mentioned by Jesus to His disciples. Later, through the inspiration of the Holy Spirit, Paul explained the concept to the new

Christians in the Grecian city of Thessalonica. They were worried about dying *before* Christ returned, so Paul offered them this comforting promise:

> *And now, brothers and sisters, I want you to know what will happen to the Christians who have died so you will not be full of sorrow like people who have no hope. For since we believe that Jesus died and was raised to life again, we also believe that when Jesus comes, God will bring back with Jesus all the Christians who have died. I can tell you this directly from the Lord: We who are still living when the Lord returns will not rise to meet him ahead of those who are in their graves. For the Lord himself will come down from heaven with a commanding shout, with the call of the archangel, and with the trumpet call of God. First, all the Christians who have died will rise from their graves. Then, together with them, we who are still alive and remain on the earth will be caught up in the clouds to meet the Lord in the air and remain with him forever* (1 Thessalonians 4:13-17).

The new believers in the church at Corinth were also puzzled about what happens when a Christian dies. Without calling the event "the rapture," Paul explained the transformation process which will happen at that time:

> *What I am saying, dear brothers and sisters, is that flesh and blood cannot inherit the Kingdom of God. These perishable bodies of ours are not able to live forever. But let me tell you a wonderful secret God*

has revealed to us. Not all of us will die, but we will all be transformed. It will happen in a moment, in the blinking of an eye, when the last trumpet is blown. For when the trumpet sounds, the Christians who have died will be raised with transformed bodies. And then we who are living will be transformed so that we will never die. For our perishable earthly bodies must be transformed into heavenly bodies that will never die (1 Corinthians 15:50-53).

"Will Pets Be Raptured?"

We doubt if you are going to see Bowser, Duke, or Snowflake shooting up to heaven when Christians are raptured. The Bible talks about the rapture happening to those who believe in Jesus. Since animals don't have an eternal soul, you shouldn't expect to see your pet in heaven.

But if you are an animal lover, don't despair. Some Bible scholars believe that animals will be in heaven because they were part of God's original creative design in the Garden of Eden. Because God gave mankind dominion over the animal kingdom (Genesis 1:28), maybe there will be pets in heaven. But since heaven is a perfect place, we suspect that there will be no yelping or scratching (and all pets will be mansion-broken).

The Sequence of Events

These two explanations give a pretty detailed account of what will happen at the rapture for all of the Christians—those living at the time and those who previously died:

✓ Christ will come down from heaven with a shout.

✓ He will bring with Him the spirits of all the Christians who have died.

✓ The voice of the archangel will be heard.

✓ At the second trumpet blast, the bodies of all Christians who have died will be raised from the grave, but these will be new, transformed bodies. The eternal spirit of the once-dead Christians will be united with their new resurrection bodies.

✓ The Christians who are still living at the time of the rapture will never experience death. Their earthly bodies will be transformed into new resurrection bodies.

✓ The previously dead Christians and the living Christians will have a brief reunion in the sky, and then they will proceed upward to join Christ Himself.

GETTING OUT OF THIS WORLD
WITHOUT DYING

The Christians who are alive at the time of the rapture won't have to die to leave this planet. They get a nonstop, direct-flight ticket. They aren't the first ones to get this privilege, however. In the Old Testament, you can read about Enoch, who was snatched off the earth by God and taken directly into heaven (Genesis 5:23); and then there was the prophet Elijah, who rose into the sky in a fiery chariot (2 Kings 2:11). But those two guys are the exceptions to the rule. So if you plan on escaping death, you had better be a Christian when the rapture occurs.

The Anatomy of the Resurrection Body

The Bible is not very specific about the options and features that will be available on the new and improved resurrection body that is given to Christians at the time of the rapture. We know that those bodies will be different, but different *how?*

We can get some clues by looking at the resurrection body of Jesus. Paul said that our new bodies would be like that of Jesus:

> *He will take these weak mortal bodies of ours and change them into glorious bodies like his own, using the same mighty power that he will use to conquer everything, everywhere* (Philippians 3:21).

Here are some of the facts we know about the new resurrected body Christ had after He rose from the grave:

✓ *His body had a human shape.* He wasn't shaped like Casper the ghost. He looked like a human. Several people didn't recognize Him at first, but they all thought He was human.

✓ *He retained His individual identity.* Mary recognized Him by His voice (John 20:16). He was recognized by sight on many other occasions. These facts suggest that our new bodies will look similar to our current ones.

✓ *His body was solid.* He was no flimsy wisp of vapor, like a hologram. People hugged Him and touched Him. His body had substance.

✓ *He ate food.* The Bible doesn't say that He got hungry, but He did share a meal with other people after His resurrection.

✓ *His body could dematerialize.* Here's something that is kind of fun to think about. Once, Jesus suddenly appeared in the middle of a room that had a closed door. Somehow, His body could travel invisibly, pass through the walls, and then appear at His choosing.

Sad to Say, Some Will Stay

But there is a very important fact you need to remember about the rapture: It only happens to Christians—those who have made an affirmative,

"Will Our Resurrected Bodies Look Younger?"

Some very knowledgeable Bible scholars believe it is possible that older people will have resurrected bodies that look younger—possibly about 30 years of age. This theory is based on the fact that Old Testament prophets couldn't begin their ministry until that age, and Christ was about 30 years old during His earthly ministry.

intentional decision to believe in Jesus Christ. When all of the Christians are raptured off the face of the earth, people left behind will be those who don't believe in Christ or didn't accept Him when they had the chance. How will they respond to all of the

THE BLIND LEADING THE BLIND

There will be a lot of used Bibles lying around after the rapture. They will be in the empty homes and churches of the Christians who have been snatched up to heaven. The people left behind will probably be scrambling to find these Bibles and to look for answers. But the people who have a real understanding of the Bible will be gone. The only "religious experts" left on earth will be the ones who were too foolish to believe God's plan in the first place.

"What About the Old Testament Saints?"

GLAD YOU ASKED

The folks from the Old Testament who believed in God will *not* be part of the rapture. The "dead in Christ" are the only ones who rise from their graves during the rapture. The Old Testament people who believed in God and were faithful to Him will rise from the dead during a 75-day period between the end of the Tribulation and the beginning of the millennium. See Daniel 12:11-12 and chapter 8 of this book.

Christians being gone? Won't it be obvious that the world is ending and the predictions of the Bible are true? Won't everyone automatically want to become a Christian?

Not all those left behind will be people who have rejected God. Many may never have heard about God's plan of salvation. When the rapture happens, if they haven't yet said "no" to God, they may still have the chance to respond *after* the rapture. The shock of the rapture will most likely cause many of these people to accept Christ.

One thing is certain: All those left behind will have tough times ahead of them.

Three Views of When

Wouldn't you like to know when the rapture is going to occur? So would we! But only God knows the date, and He isn't telling. Here's what Jesus said when His disciples asked Him for a timetable of the end of the world.

> *"The Father sets those dates," he replied, "and they are not for you to know"* (Acts 1:7).

So there is no way to know the exact date. It could happen at any time. In fact, Christians in the first

---

Y2K HYSTERIA

You've probably noticed that we haven't yet talked about "Y2K"—which stands for "Year 2000." Well, we're only going to deal with it once, and we're going to do it in this little box! It's not that Y2K isn't an important issue. Everyone from corporate CEOs to computer experts to religious leaders have offered their vision of what's going to happen when the clock strikes midnight in the year 2000. On one end of the spectrum people are saying that we will notice some temporary inconveniences in the way we do business. One the other end, some pundits, such as our friend Hal Lindsey, are saying that "Y2K is a logic bomb that could do to our civilization what the iceberg did to the Titanic."

Our take on Y2K is that we need to be wise about potential problems, but not panic because we're afraid the world is going to end. And we should certainly avoid thinking that such an event is going to trigger the rapture.

"What's Holding Things Up?"

If the Christians in the first century were expecting the rapture to happen at any time and certainly during their lifetime, you might think that God's plan hit some sort of snag. Has He gotten off schedule? Well, try looking at things from God's perspective. Remember that He doesn't operate on the same time continuum that we do. The apostle Peter explained it this way:

> *But you must not forget, dear friends, that a day is like a thousand years to the Lord, and a thousand years is like a day. The Lord isn't really being slow about his promise to return, as some people think. No, he is being patient for your sake. He does not want anyone to perish, so he is giving more time for everyone to repent. But the day of the Lord will come as unexpectedly as a thief (2 Peter 3:8-10).*

century were expecting that it would happen in their lifetime. After Paul had explained the concept of the rapture to the Christians in the Thessalonica church, he added these words about its timing:

> *I really don't need to write to you about how and when all this will happen, for you know quite well that the day of the Lord will come unexpectedly, like a thief in the night (1 Thessalonians 5:1,2).*

A Word About the Tribulation

Excuse us while we interrupt ourselves for a moment. We'll explain the tribulation in detail in chapter 7. For this discussion, let's just say that it is a seven-year period that clearly marks the beginning of the end. There will be increasing worldwide trouble during these seven years, caused by natural disasters and by Satan. It will be a time of terrible suffering and torture. The climax will be the battle of Armageddon, which will be interrupted by Christ returning to earth (the second coming) with all of the Christians to establish peace on earth for 1000 years (the millennium).

Bible scholars concede that we can't know the exact date of the rapture, but there is still a great debate over where the rapture falls in the overall sequence of end-of-the-world events. There are three major views, and they all pertain to the timing of the rapture in relation to the tribulation.

Whenever people talk about the rapture in the context of the end of the world, they put it in one of three positions: at the start of the tribulation, in the middle of the tribulation, or at the end of the tribulation.

The "Pre-trib" View—the Rapture Starts It All

Many people believe that the rapture will be the big event that signals the beginning of the tribulation.

After all, it will be pretty obvious when it happens. Proponents of this "pre-trib" view make the following arguments for their position:

1. The rapture will happen first so that Christians can escape the horrors of the tribulation. Among the verses used to support this point are:

> *Because you have obeyed my command to persevere, I will protect you from the great time of testing that will come upon the whole world to test those who belong to this world* (Revelation 3:10).

> *For God decided to save us through our Lord Jesus Christ, not to pour out his anger on us* (1 Thessalonians 5:9).

This view holds that the wrath of the tribulation is designed exclusively for those who rejected God (and not for Christians).

2. Jesus suggested that we pray to escape tribulation. As He was describing the calamities which would happen at the end of the world, Jesus told His disciples to "pray that, if possible, you may escape these horrors" (Luke 21:36).

3. There is no specific mention of "the church" during the tribulation. Chapters 1–3 of Revelation mention Christians (collectively referred to as "the church"). Pre-trib proponents argue that since the church is in heaven in chapter 4, it cannot be on earth during the tribulation events described in Revelation 5 and following.

4. Christians are specifically told to expect the rapture. Take a good look at passages such as 1 Corinthians 15, 1 Thessalonians 4–5, Titus 2, and 2 Peter 3. These admonitions of Paul and Peter that believers should anticipate the rapture suggest that it must be the first event to occur. Pre-trib proponents also argue that the rapture wouldn't be a surprise if it came at the end of the tribulation, as it could be anticipated and calculated by those events.

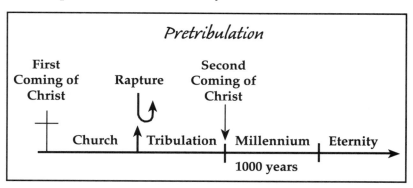

Pretribulation

As you can expect, this pre-trib view has great appeal with Christians because they don't want to be hanging around during the tribulation.

The "Mid-trib" View—Half and Half

Some scholars adhere to the position that the rapture will occur at the midpoint of the tribulation. As you will see in the next chapter, the seven-year tribulation will have two distinct phases. The first 3 ½ years will be a time when the world is lulled into a sense of false peace, but in the next 3 ½ years everything will fall apart and the wickedness of the world leader (the Antichrist) will be revealed. Proponents of the mid-trib viewpoint contend that Christians will be around until the halfway mark. The following verse is often used to explain that the tribulation will be "shortened" for Christians:

> *For that will be a time of greater horror than anything the world has ever seen or will ever see again. In fact, unless that time of calamity is shortened, the entire human race will be destroyed. But it will be shortened for the sake of God's chosen ones* (Matthew 24:21,22).

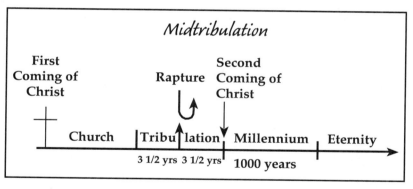

The "Post-trib" View—It Ain't Over Till It's Over

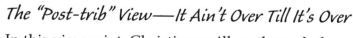

In this viewpoint, Christians will go through the entire seven-year tribulation. The rapture won't happen until immediately before the second coming. Since the rapture and second coming are separate

events, here is how it plays out under this theory:
The Christians (living and dead) will be swooped up
in resurrected bodies to meet Jesus in the sky ("the
rapture"), and then they will all parade down to
earth together to establish Christ's kingdom ("the
second coming"). The rapture and second coming
will be separate events, but will happen in immediate
succession.

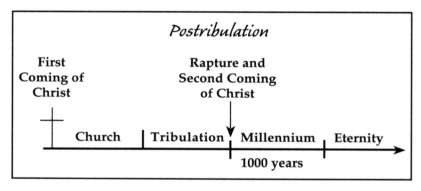

Post-trib proponents seem to be divided on whether
Christians will actually suffer during the tribulation.

**Some say that Christians will be protected
from calamity.** God is certainly able to do this. In the
Old Testament, He spared Noah from the flood and
protected the Israelite slaves from many of the
plagues that bombarded Pharaoh and the Egyptians.
Also, as you'll read in the next chapter, there will be
144,000 witnesses who are going to be spared from
suffering during the tribulation. So it is no problem
for God if He wants to protect the Christians from the
trials of the tribulation.

Some say that Christians will suffer along with everyone else. Why should it be any different *now* than it was *then*? While Christians in the United

---

So, If I Die Before The Rapture . . . ?

If the rapture happens while you are still alive, you will either be sucked up off the earth to be with Jesus or you will be left behind.

But what if you die before the rapture? Well, your physical body is buried or cremated, and the deterioration process will begin. But what about your "soul"—that eternal part of you that never dies? On this eternally significant question, we've got good news and bad news.

If you rejected Christ during your lifetime, then your soul hangs out in torment, awaiting your final judgment and sentence to hell.

If you established a relationship with Christ during your lifetime, then your soul goes immediately into God's presence. The Bible seems to indicate that you'll be in a terrific place (referred to as "paradise") which is like a waiting room for heaven. After the rapture your soul will be rejoined with your new and improved resurrected body.

Go to page 243 for another discussion on this fascinating topic.

Chapter 9

States don't really *suffer* very much because of their faith, Christians in other countries around the world are being tortured and murdered for claiming the name of Christ. If God has allowed Christians to suffer persecution during the course of the last 2000 years, He may choose to have them suffer during the tribulation as well. After all, suffering and hardship should be an expected part of life for the Christian.

✓ *. . . here on earth you will have many trials and sorrows . . .* (John 16:33)

✓ *. . . enter into the Kingdom of God through many tribulations . . .* (Acts 14:22)

✓ *. . . we run into problems and trials . . .* (Romans 5:3)

✓ *. . . to keep you from becoming disturbed by the troubles you were going through . . .* (1 Thessalonians 3:3)

✓ *. . . in Jesus we are partners in suffering . . .* (Revelation 1:9)

What Does All This Mean to You?

Don't let the "pre-trib/mid-trib/post-trib" debate distract you. You could spend a lifetime researching and arguing the fine points of the timing of the rapture. Many people have. You could easily get so bogged down that you won't see the rapture through the research. There are capable scholars to support each of the major views. We have our opinions, but that isn't important either.

Just know that the rapture *is* going to happen. And follow the biblical instructions to expect it, living your life in anticipation of it.

"What's That Again?"

1. The rapture is the event when Jesus is reunited with all Christians, living and dead. He will return in the sky (without actually touching earth). The bodies of the Christians who previously died will be resurrected from their graves; their eternal spirits will be joined with these new bodies. The Christians who are living at the time of the rapture will also have their bodies transformed. The new bodies of the resurrected Christians and the living Christians will be lifted into the sky and they will be with Jesus forever.

2. If a person did not have an opportunity to respond to God before the rapture (had, for example, never heard about God's plan of salvation), it won't be too late. Probably many of these people will respond positively to God, because the events of the rapture will be convincing proof that God knows what He is talking about!

3. The new body that a Christian receives at the rapture will have both human characteristics and supernatural features.

4. Many people believe that the rapture will occur before the beginning of the tribulation ("pre-trib"). Others believe that it will take place in the middle of the tribulation ("mid-trib"). Still others take the position that it will occur at the end of the tribulation ("post-trib").

Dig Deeper

When the Trumpet Sounds edited by Thomas Ice and Timothy Demy. Twenty-one prophecy experts give their views on the rapture.

Three Views on the Rapture. In this unique approach, three different Bible scholars one by one present their views on the pre-, mid-, and post-tribulational rapture. Then the other two scholars respond to each presentation. Fascinating!

Come Quickly, Lord Jesus by Charles C. Ryrie. This book, which presents a premillenial, pre-tribulational view, explores the key events that will surround the rapture.

The Final Drama by John Walvoord. Dr. Walvoord has done more to support the premillennial view than anyone else in the last half-century. In this book he explains the scriptural guidelines he uses to interpret the rapture and all other end-times events.

Left Behind by Tim LaHaye and Jerry Jenkins. These two guys have teamed up to write a series of novels on the end times (and judging by the tremendous response, they have struck a chord with readers). The first book in the series concerns the rapture. The main character, airline pilot Rayford Steele, is one of those "left behind." His primary goal is to search for the truth. Stay tuned!

Moving On . . .

So much for the Christians who have left planet Earth. Perhaps you are wondering about those who get left behind. That's exactly what we're going to look at in the next chapter: What is happening down here on earth as the world gets closer to its end? If the rapture ride in the sky isn't enough motivation for you, then we're sure that the events of "the tribulation" are going to convince you that this planet is no place to be hanging around when the end gets near.

Chapter 7

The Tribulation: Going from Bad to Worse

This is a wonderful world. It may destroy itself, but you'll be able to watch it all on TV.

—*Bob Hope*

BRUCE & STAN SAY

If a scary movie tends to keep you awake at night, then be sure to read this chapter early in the morning. We aren't kidding. In this chapter, we're going to review the events which the Bible says will mark the end of the world. As you'll see, it would be an understatement to describe these events as horrible. It's going to be like nothing the world has ever known before.

This has been a difficult chapter for us to write. If you haven't noticed, we have a pretty easygoing style, but there is no "easy going" in a discussion about the tribulation. It is grim. But this is information that you have to know . . . because the Bible says that it *is* going to happen.

So take a deep breath and brace yourself. We are sure that what you are about to read will change the way you think about the future. And we are also sure that this chapter will change the way you think about your life *right now.*

Bruce & Stan

Chapter 7

The Tribulation: Going from Bad to Worse

What's Ahead

➤ Who says? . . . Jesus, that's who
➤ Seven years of hell on earth (literally)
➤ The Antichrist: Satan's puppet
➤ Armageddon—the Bible version
➤ What does all of this mean to you?

*I*n the last chapter, we discussed "the rapture"—
that amazing event when Christians are going to
be sucked off the earth to join Jesus in the sky. But
the end-times events described in the Bible are not
restricted to people who believe and follow Jesus.
Everyone everywhere will be a participant in these
events—whether they want to be or not.

Who Says? . . . Jesus, That's Who

If you have a fascination about how the world (as we
know it) is going to end, you are in good company.
So did the disciples of Jesus. They couldn't contain
their curiosity, so one day they simply asked Him:

> *Will there be any sign ahead of time to signal your
> return and the end of the world?* (Matthew 24:3).

181

So if you are looking for clues to the end of the world, we suggest that the most reliable source is Jesus, the Son of God. Here is a short list of what He told His disciples would be the signs that the end is at hand (you can read for yourself in Matthew 24:1-22; Mark 13:3-23; and Luke 21:5-28):

✓ International wars

✓ Revolutions

✓ Famines

✓ Earthquakes

✓ Epidemics

✓ Strange natural disasters

✓ Unpredictable oceanic events

✓ Worldwide dissemination of the message of Jesus

✓ Persecution of Christians

✓ Rampant immorality

Jesus summed up the effect of all these calamities with this statement:

For that will be a time of greater horror than anything the world has ever seen or will ever see again (Matthew 24:21).

TRIBULATION WITH A CAPITAL "T"

The period of worldwide horror which Jesus predicted would occur at the end of the world is known as the tribulation. Don't confuse this reference with tribulations—the kind of hardships suffered by people in their day-to-day lives (as in "I've been going through a lot of trials and tribulations").

As discussed below, the tribulation will last for seven years, and the last half will be much worse than the first half. Some scholars refer to the entire seven-year period as the "Great Tribulation," while other scholars only use that terminology for the last 3 ½ years (because that period of time will be the worst).

The Vision and Prophecy of Daniel

Jesus wasn't the only one to predict that cataclysmic events would occur at the end of the world. Back in Old Testament times, around 550 B.C., the prophet Daniel had visions concerning how the world was going to end. Here is his description:

> *Then there will be a time of anguish greater than any since nations first came into existence* (Daniel 12:1).

His prophecies include the same sort of disasters which Jesus predicted:

"When Will the Tribulation Start?"

GLAD YOU ASKED

Daniel says that the seven-year tribulation will start when the nation of Israel signs a peace treaty with the Antichrist (Daniel 9:27). We don't know who the Antichrist will be, but we do know that the treaty will be for seven years. Until about 50 years ago, this prophecy seemed unlikely to be fulfilled, as there was no nation of Israel. In 1948, however, Israel became a nation. Many scholars believe that the national status of Israel was the last piece of the puzzle. With all of the political and military unrest in the Middle East, it is easy to imagine that a world leader (the Antichrist) could negotiate a peace treaty between Israel and its neighbors. We'll give you more information about the Antichrist beginning on page 192.

✓ One-half of the world's population will be killed.
✓ The earth will be severely damaged by natural and man-made disasters.
✓ There will be earthquakes, disease, and warfare.
✓ Humanity will be close to extinction.

Daniel's prophecies, along with the statements of Jesus and the Book of Revelation, form the foundation of what we know about the tribulation. It is Daniel's prophecies which reveal to us that the tribulation is going to last for seven years (see the "Daniel's Calendar of 70 Sets of 7" box below).

DANIEL'S CALENDAR OF 70 SETS OF 7

Daniel refers in his prophecy to "seventy sets of seven" (Daniel 9:24-27). Some older Bible translations refer to 70 "weeks," but the overwhelming consensus of scholars is that these references refer to 70 sets of 7 years—or a total of 490 years. The prophecies of Daniel indicate that the first 483 years lead up to the crucifixion of Christ—that the clock stops running during the "church age"—and that the last 7 years start ticking during the tribulation, so that the buzzer rings at the second coming of Christ when He returns to earth to establish His kingdom.

More than 500 years before Christ was born, Daniel predicted that 69 sets of 7 (483 years) would pass between the time that a decree was made to rebuild the temple in Jerusalem and the time when "the anointed one" would be "cut off." When Daniel wrote this prophecy, he was living in exile in Babylon, and the temple in Jerusalem had been demolished by the invading Assyrians. Historians tell us that after Daniel's death on March 5, 444 B.C., the Persian king Artaxerxes issued a decree that the temple in Jerusalem could be rebuilt. Exactly 173,880 days later (which is 483 years using a 360-day calendar), on Larch 30, A.D. 33, Jesus entered the city of Jerusalem on a donkey in the event known as Palm Sunday (which was the prelude to His crucifixion).

According to Daniel's timetable, we have just seven more years to go until the second coming, and the clock will start ticking (at the beginning of the tribulation) as soon as Israel signs the peace treaty with the as-yet unidentified Antichrist.

There's Tribulation in John's Revelation, Too

Much of the information about the tribulation is found in Revelation, the last book of the Bible.This book contains the writings of the disciple John when he was exiled by Roman authorities to the island of Patmos off the coast of Asia about 95 A.D. In the Book of Revelation, John recounts the vision which God gave him about the end of the world. Chapters 4–19 of Revelation contain very detailed and specific predictions about the events of the tribulation.

Seven Years of Hell on Earth (Literally)

Revelation is a confusing book for many people (Bruce and Stan included). Most Bible scholars agree that it contains symbolic as well as literal references. The trick is figuring out which is which. For example, in his discussion of the events of the tribulation, John describes a great scroll with seven seals, and then angels blowing trumpets, and then a bunch of bowls. Each of the seals, trumpets, and bowls seems to be symbolic, but the events that they describe are certainly meant to be taken literally.

The horror of the seals, trumpets, and bowls represents the beginning of God's judgment upon a world that has rejected Him. These cata-strophic events begin at the commencement of the tribulation and continue through the seven-year period.

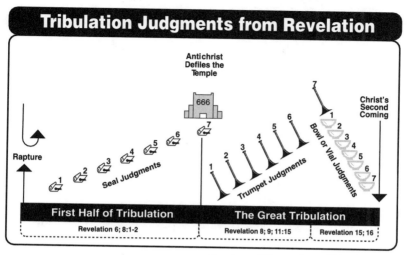

Courtesy of Thomas Ice and Timothy Demy

The Judgment of the Seven Seals

In Revelation 6:1–8:6, John tells of a vision in which he saw a Lamb (a reference to Jesus Christ) sitting on the throne of God. The Lamb opened a scroll, and with the breaking of each of the seven seals, John sees a particular vision with specific meaning for the end times.

"How Can a Loving God Be So Mean?"

Does the severity of these judgments upon the earth seem to be inconsistent with your image of a "loving God"? We have two suggestions which might help you understand what is going on here. First, don't focus on just one aspect of God's personality. Sure, He is a loving God (and John 3:16 proves this). But He is also a holy and just God. His righteousness demands that sin and rebellion be punished. Secondly, we can't even begin to understand what is "fair" from God's perspective. Although we may not always understand (or agree) with His methods, we should remember that He is perfect and can do nothing wrong.

	John's Vision	*Representing*
First Seal (Rev. 6:1,2)	A rider on a white horse	Most Bible scholars interpret the rider to be the Antichrist.
Second Seal (Rev. 6:3,4)	A rider on a red horse	The bloodshed from war on earth
Third Seal (Rev. 6:5,6)	A rider on a black horse	Famine
Fourth Seal (Rev. 6:7,8)	A rider on a green horse	One-fourth of the world's population dies from warfare, famine, and disease.
Fifth Seal (Rev. 6:9-11)	Souls under the altar	Those who were martyred for the sake of Christ
Sixth Seal (Rev. 6:12-17)	Natural calamities	People are gripped with fear and hide for safety in caves.

Here is John's description of what happens at the breaking of the seventh seal:

> *When the Lamb broke the seventh seal, there was silence throughout heaven for about half an hour. And I saw the seven angels who stand before God, and they were given seven trumpets* (Revelation 8:1,2).

The Judgment of the Seven Trumpets

John's vision continues with the angels blowing the trumpets in Revelation 8:7–11:19. With the blast of each trumpet, John sees an event which impacts earth's inhabitants:

	The Event	*The Impact*
First Trumpet (Rev. 8:7)	Hail and fire (with blood).	One-third of the earth's vegetation is destroyed.
Second Trumpet (Rev. 8:8,9)	A burning mountain drops into the sea.	One-third of the sea becomes blood; one-third of sea animals die; one-third of all ships are destroyed.
Third Trumpet (Rev. 8:10,11)	Star falls from the sky.	One-third of drinking water becomes contaminated; many die from poisoning.
Fourth Trumpet (Rev. 8:12)	Heavenly bodies collide.	One-third of earth's light is lost.
Fifth Trumpet (Rev. 9:1-12)	Poisonous locusts attack people.	People suffer painful torture for five months.
Sixth Trumpet (Rev. 9:13-21)	Two hundred million horsemen attack.	One-third of mankind is killed.

Then with the blast of the seventh and final trumpet, these horrible events come to a conclusion. There is then a time when God is worshiped in heaven, before a great earthquake hits the earth (Revelation 11:15-19).

The Judgment of the Seven Bowls

While the world is still reeling from the disasters of the seven seals and seven trumpets, the final set of God's judgments begins. Here is how John describes it:

> *Then I saw in heaven another significant event, and it was great and marvelous. Seven angels were holding the seven last plagues, which would bring God's wrath to completion.... Then I heard a mighty voice shouting from the Temple to the seven angels, "Now go your ways and empty out the seven bowls of God's wrath on the earth"* (Revelation 15:1; 16:1).

Here is what will happen when these "bowls" of God's wrath are poured out on the earth:

First Bowl   Horrible, malignant sores will break out on anyone who has the "mark of the beast" and has worshiped his statue (Revelation 16:2).

Second Bowl   The oceans turn to blood, and everything in them dies (Revelation 16:3).

Third Bowl   The earth's rivers and springs turn to blood (Revelation 16:4).

The End of the World According to Hollywood

The Road Warrior (and its predecessor, *Mad Max*) depict what the earth will be like in the postnuclear explosion future: lots of desolation, and a few marauding gangs of outlaw bikers, with a young Mel Gibson as the world's only hope. Even Mel can't make the future look bright.

Fourth Bowl	The heat from the sun intensifies, and everyone is scorched (Revelation 16:8,9).
Fifth Bowl	The earth is plunged into darkness, and everyone is in anguish from their sores and pain (Revelation 16:10,11).
Sixth Bowl	The Euphrates River dries up—a geological event which allows armies from the east to march toward Israel. The world leaders, under demonic influence, prepare for world war (Revelation 16:12-16).
Seventh Bowl	The world experiences its greatest earthquake—cities around the world are just heaps of rubble, islands disappear, and mountains are leveled. The earth is hit with its most severe hailstorm—hailstones weighing 75 pounds hit earth's inhabitants (Revelation 16:17-21).

The Antichrist: Satan's Puppet

Meanwhile, in the midst of all the disasters from the judgments of seals, trumpets, and bowls, Satan is hard at work on planet Earth. He has always been trying to thwart God's plan and sucker people into disbelieving the obvious evidence of God's existence. During the tribulation, Satan will intensify his efforts. (If the rapture happens immediately before the tribulation—the "pre-trib view"—then all of the Christians, and the power of the Holy Spirit that

You Do the Math

More than half of the earth's population will be killed during the judgments of the tribulation. Under the fourth seal, 25 percent of the world's population will be killed. That will only leave 75 percent. Then, under the sixth trumpet, another one-third of the world's population will be killed in battle. That means only 50 percent of the population is left before the beginning of the judgments of the seven bowls.

resides inside them, will be removed from earth and Satan's scheme will be easier to achieve.)

Remember John's vision of the first seal? When it broke, he saw a rider on a white horse (Revelation 6:1,2). Many Bible scholars see this as a clear reference to "the Antichrist." The Antichrist will be Satan's stooge during the tribulation. But don't let our derogatory comment about the Antichrist lead you to suspect that he is a goofball like Larry, Moe, or Curley. Just the opposite. All indications are that he will be a smooth, debonair political leader who will be able to persuade most of the world to follow him.

The sequence of Satan's schemes for the tribulation can be traced by reading the predictions of Jesus, Daniel, and John. We'll blend them together for the sake of continuity.

The First Half of the Tribulation—the Antichrist Is a Great Impostor

Remember that the rapture will probably be the triggering event for the tribulation. That would make sense, because the worldwide confusion that follows the disappearance of all the Christians would leave the citizens of planet Earth in a state of panic. This creates the perfect opportunity for a political leader to emerge who could have global support. The Antichrist is just such a figure, and he plays a key role in the tribulation. Here is how the scenario plays out:

- ✓ The Antichrist serves as a mediator between the Arabs and Israel. He takes the side of the Jews in claiming that the land of Palestine belongs to the nation of Israel. The Antichrist is instrumental in negotiating a peace treaty with the nation of Israel and its Arab neighbors. The signing of the seven-year peace treaty will mark the beginning of the tribulation (Daniel 9:26,27).

- ✓ The Antichrist rises in popularity, becoming a leader in the ten-nation confederacy that will end up ruling the world during the tribulation (Daniel 2:42-44; Revelation 12:3; 13:1; 17:12,16).

- ✓ With a false sense of security from the peace treaty, Israel rebuilds the temple in Jerusalem. The whole system of ritual sacrifices is reinstituted by the Jews (Revelation 11:1,2).

- ✓ There are 144,000 Jews (12,000 from each of the 12 tribes of Israel) who become Christians and

PROFILE OF THE ANTICHRIST

There is not enough information about the Antichrist to predict who he is or where he will come from. (Scholars disagree as to whether he will be a Jew or a Gentile.) But we do know that he will be a dangerous fraud. Referring to the Antichrist as "the man of lawlessness," Paul said this about him:

This evil man will come to do the work of Satan with counterfeit power and signs and miracles. He will use every kind of wicked deception to fool those who are on their way to destruction because they refuse to believe the truth that would save them (2 Thessalonians 2:9,10).

spread the message of Jesus Christ around the world during the tribulation (Revelation 7).

✓ God appoints two people to be His special witnesses to the Jews in Jerusalem and in Israel. They preach about God's salvation, which is available only through belief in Jesus Christ. God supernaturally empowers these "two witnesses" to perform miracles which bring credibility to their claims (Revelation 11:3-6).

The Second Half of the Tribulation—the Antichrist Reveals His True Nature

Halfway through the tribulation, at the 3½-year mark, things change drastically when the Antichrist drops his charade and reveals his true evil nature.

The Aliases of the Antichrist

We can get a glimpse into the true nature of the Antichrist if we look at the names by which the Bible refers to him. He is also known as:

✓ A fierce king (Daniel 8:23)

✓ A master of intrigue (Daniel 8:23)

✓ A despicable man (Daniel 11:21)

✓ A worthless shepherd (Zechariah 11:17)

✓ The man of lawlessness (2 Thessalonians 2:3)

✓ The evil man (2 Thessalonians 2:9)

✓ The beast (Revelation 11:7)

✓ The Antichrist breaks his treaty with Israel, and the Jews are the subject of great persecution (Daniel 9:27; Isaiah 28:18).

✓ The Antichrist is killed, but he is raised back to life by the power of Satan, in an attempt to counterfeit the resurrection of Jesus Christ (Revelation 13:3,4).

Pin the Tale on the Antichrist

For almost 2000 years, people have been telling the tale of the Antichrist and trying to guess his identity. So far, all the guesses have proven incorrect. Here are a few examples of past candidates:

Nero. Roman emperors were always likely suspects. Nowadays, it doesn't look like the Antichrist will turn out to be an Italian guy wearing a toga, with a wreath on his head.

The Pope. At the time of the Reformation, some Protestants thought that the Pope was the Antichrist. Just to balance things out, the Roman Catholics said the same thing about Martin Luther.

Adolf Hitler. We agree that he was a dominant, demented world leader. But he is dead now. Or even if he managed to escape the bombing of his bunker and is living in exile in Argentina, he would be over 110 years old. Also, in our present culture, nobody is going to follow a guy with such a dorky mustache.

More recently, we can add Henry Kissinger, Saddam Hussein, and Mikhail Gorbachev to the list of those put forward as the Antichrist. We can even make our own *wrong* predictions. That's not hard, and it's kind of fun. For example, here are three of Bruce and Stan's "sure to be wrong" predictions of the Antichrist's identity:

Johnny Carson. Accompanied by his faithful sidekick, Ed McMahon (the "false prophet"), Johnny will start his comeback on cable channel 666.

Oprah Winfrey. She will initiate her plan for economic world domination through a strategy of commercial endorsements on all products—ranging from her own line of perfume ("Oprah Odors") to breakfast cereal ("Oprah Oaties").

Bill Gates. Watch for this subtle clue: All Microsoft software programs will require a redesigned mouse pointing devise, called "the beast," and the flashing cursor on the monitor will be referred to as "the mark of the beast."

✓ After his death and resurrection, the Antichrist carries out the assassination of the leaders of three countries in the confederacy. The leaders of the other countries immediately relinquish their power and position to the Antichrist. He is now perfectly situated to carry out Satan's plan for world domination. More and more, the world moves toward a single government and economy (Daniel 7:24; Revelation 17:12,13).

✓ In a public display, the two witnesses are murdered by the Antichrist for their allegiance to God. Their dead corpses are left in the street as an example for the world to see. However, after 3½ days, the two witnesses are resurrected by the power of God and are taken to heaven in the sight of the entire world (Revelation 11:7-13).

✓ The Antichrist puts himself forward as a god and demands the worship and adoration of the people of the world (Revelation 13:3,4,8).

✓ Satan empowers "the false prophet" to be the Antichrist's sidekick. Through demonic miracles, the false prophet creates an entire religion around worshiping the Antichrist, which is really worship of Satan (Revelation 13:11-15).

✓ The false prophet administers the issuance of the "mark of the beast" (some form of identification placed on the forehead or right hand by which people display their allegiance to the Antichrist). Without this identification, no one can buy or sell in the world's economy (Revelation 13:16-18).

"What Is the 'Mark of the Beast'?"

In past decades, people thought the "mark of the beast" might have to be some sort of tattoo. More recently, ATM cards have opened up new possibilities. But you shouldn't limit your thinking to a tattoo or an identification card. Present technology is already way beyond that. Currently, we can identify people by using voice prints or laser scans of their retina. Scientists have even developed a computer chip small enough to be imbedded in your fingertip. With such technology under the control of the Antichrist, complete power over world commerce would be possible.

✓ The Antichrist sets himself up in the temple in Jerusalem and performs perverse acts of desecration (Daniel 9:27; Matthew 24:15,16; 2 Thessalonians 2:4).

✓ The Antichrist attempts to annihilate every Jew. It may be Satan's belief that he can divert God's plan for the world if the Jews are eliminated (Revelation 12:1-6).

✓ The Antichrist leads a military alliance of the western world powers. They prepare to battle against a mighty army of 200 million soldiers from the east in the "battle of Armageddon" (Daniel 11:40-45; Revelation 16:14-16).

666

Here is all anyone knows for sure about the "mark of the beast":

> *Wisdom is needed to understand this. Let the one who has understanding solve the number of the beast, for it is the number of a man. His number is 666* (Revelation 13:18).

People have tried to determine the identity of the Antichrist through the number 666. Some people assign numerical values to letters of the alphabet, trying to see what name has the sum of 666. For example, assigning values from A=1 to Z=26, then the name "Bruce and Stan" would total 122. So you can eliminate us from the Antichrist sweepstakes.

Armageddon—the Bible Version

 The last event of the tribulation is the battle of Armageddon. This battle was predicted by Daniel, John, and other Old Testament prophets (see Joel 3:9-17 and Zechariah 14:1-3). The battlefield will be a large plain in northern Israel. Because the land of Palestine and the capital city of Jerusalem will become the center of world power by the end of the tribulation, it is not surprising that the final battle of the ages will occur here.

Armageddon is going to be a battle unlike anything the world has ever known. At the same time, military powers from the four corners of the globe will converge upon Israel to battle for world domination. There is not a single set of verses which describes the events in consecutive order, but Dr. Arnold Fruchtenbaum has compiled the various Armageddon passages of the Bible to arrive at this sequence of events:

1. *The Antichrist's allies assemble.* The ten-nation confederacy assembles with the intent to wipe the Jews off the map (Revelation 16:12-16).

2. *Babylon is destroyed.* While the Antichrist is with his armies at Armageddon, the invading forces from the east destroy his capital city of Babylon, which is in present-day Iran (Jeremiah 50–51; Revelation 18).

3. *Jerusalem falls.* Instead of moving eastward to protect his capital city of Babylon, the Antichrist will move his forces south to the city of Jerusalem. The Jews will resist, but the Antichrist will prevail. There will be devastating loss of life (Zechariah 12:1-3; 14:1,2).

4. *The Antichrist moves south against the remnant.* After he has captured Jerusalem, the Antichrist will disperse his armies to the south in an attempt to capture and kill the Jews who are hiding in the outlying areas—"the remnant" (Jeremiah 49:13,14).

5. *The regeneration of Israel.* When the forces of the Antichrist descend on the Jews in the

---

The End of the World According to Hollywood

Armageddon. Summer would not be complete without a movie blockbuster about the end of the world. The summer of 1998 had everyone wondering whether Bruce Willis could drill a hole fast enough and deep enough into an asteroid the size of Texas. Fortunately he does, so the world is saved from being smashed into smithereens.

"Where's All the Technology?"

GLAD YOU ASKED The Bible's predictions about the end of the world give the impression of hand-to-hand combat and soldiers on horseback. With nuclear weapons and computer technology, aren't we long past these archaic methods of warfare? Well, it is quite possible that the calamities of the tribulation will destroy most of the world's technology. Another possibility is that because the Bible prophets couldn't possibly have conceptualized weaponry of the twenty-first century, they would have had to describe these events with the only terminology known to them.

wilderness, the Jews will turn back to God. Two-thirds of the Jewish population will have been killed during the tribulation, but the remaining one-third, "the remnant," will acknowledge Jesus as the Messiah (Jeremiah 3:11-18).

6. *The second coming of Jesus Christ.* The repentant Jews will plead for the Messiah to rescue them from the attacking Antichrist. Their prayers will be answered when Jesus Christ returns to earth with His angelic army and the Christian saints to battle the Antichrist (Jude 14,15; Revelation 19:11-16).

"Can People Be Saved During the Tribulation?"

Yes! Remember that the two witnesses and the 144,000 will be hard at work explaining that belief in Jesus Christ is the only way to have eternal life. In his vision of the end time, John described an event during the tribulation when multitudes worshiped God:

> *After [the commissioning of the 144,000], I saw a vast crowd, too great to count, from every nation and tribe and people and language, standing in front of the throne, and before the Lamb. They were clothed in white and held palm branches in their hands. And they were shouting with a mighty shout, "Salvation comes from our God on the throne and from the Lamb!"* (Revelation 7:9,10).

7. *The final battle.* Jesus Christ will battle alone against the Antichrist and his armies. The Antichrist will be killed and his forces will be destroyed (Habakkuk 3:13; Revelation 14:19,20).

8. *The ascent to the Mount of Olives.* At the defeat of the Antichrist and his army, there will be a tremendous earthquake and hailstorm. As these calamities subside, Christ will assume His role as rightful king

Chapter 8

and ruler of the universe on the Mount of Olives (Zechariah 14:3,4; Revelation 16:17-21).

The second coming of Christ is a tremendous event that deserves special attention, so we'll take a closer look at it in chapter 8.

"What's That Again?"

1. The tribulation is a seven-year period of disaster which will immediately precede the second coming of Christ.

2. During the tribulation, God will pour out His wrath on the earth in punishment for mankind's sin and rebellion. The catastrophes will include earthquakes, fires, famines, and other natural calamities of immeasurable proportions. More than half of the earth's population will be killed in these disasters.

3. Also during the tribulation, Satan will promote his schemes through a world leader (referred to as the Antichrist).

4. The Antichrist will eventually declare himself to be God as he asserts worldwide domination. His identifying mark (the "mark of the beast") will be required for commerce. Those without this mark will likely starve.

5. The tribulation will end in the prolonged battle of Armageddon. The conflict between the earthly armies will turn heavenward as Christ returns to earth. Christ will prevail.

Dig Deeper

Revelation Made Plain by Tim LaHaye. This is LaHaye's commentary on the Book of Revelation. LaHaye's explanation of the seal judgments, the trumpet judgments, and other symbolism in Revelation relating to the tribulation is very helpful.

The Prophecy Watch by Thomas Ice and Timothy Demy. Here is a basic overview of Bible prophecy that guides you step-by-step through the rapture, tribulation, and other end-times events.

The End by Ed Dobson. Pastor Dobson gives his views on the tribulation and what it will be like.

The Antichrist by Arthur W. Pink. A classic book which many scholars consider to be the most complete book on the Antichrist ever written.

Tribulation Force by Tim LaHaye and Jerry Jenkins. The second book in the series of end-times novels continues the dramatic story of those left behind. Our hero, Rayford Steele, and others form the Tribulation Force to fight the forces of evil during "the seven most chaotic years the planet will ever see."

Nicolae by Tim LaHaye and Jerry Jenkins. This novel (number three in the series) follows the rise of the Antichrist. Rayford Steele becomes the "ears of the tribulation saints" in the highest echelon of the Antichrist's regime.

Moving On . . .

It is time to leave the tumultuous events of the tribulation behind us. By now, you deserve to move on to something much more pleasant and tranquil. So let's focus on the victorious second coming of Christ, which will begin the 1000-year reign of Christ on earth—an earth that is the way it was meant to be.

Chapter 8

The Second Coming: Here Comes the King

We look forward to that wonderful event when the glory of our great God and Savior, Jesus Christ, will be revealed.

—*Paul the Apostle*

When you think of Jesus, what pops into your head? Do you see baby Jesus, meek and mild? Do you see a gentle, soft-spoken man who healed the sick? Do you see a broken man dying on a cross?

None of those images would be incorrect. Jesus came to earth 2000 years ago and took on the role of a servant so that He could do for us what we could never do for ourselves: die as a sacrifice in order to satisfy a holy God.

But there's another image of Jesus, quite different than Jesus the Servant, and that is Jesus the King, the conquering Warrior, the Victor who will vanquish His foes and judge the world when He comes to earth again. People don't think about this Jesus, but they should. Because Jesus the King is just as real as Jesus the Servant. In this chapter we're going to see just *how* real.

Bruce & Stan

Chapter 8

The Second Coming: Here Comes the King

What's Ahead

- The wicked plot against the godly
- It's only a matter of time
- What is the second coming?
- The nature of the second coming
- The purpose of the second coming
- The millennium: fact or fantasy?
- What does all this mean to you?

*T*hat guy gets away with murder. Have you ever said that about someone? When we use this phrase we mean that somebody is getting away with something he shouldn't. You know it. He knows it. Everybody knows it except the people in charge. Or so it seems.

These days that statement doesn't seem so figurative. People really do get away with murder. On a smaller and closer-to-home scale, people also get away with cheating, lying, and stealing. Many feel our justice system favors criminals over their victims. Sometimes it seems like the bad guys come out on top more often than the good guys do.

209

The notion that bad triumphs over good is nothing new. Three thousand years ago King David lamented the same problem:

> *I myself have seen it happen—proud and evil people thriving like mighty trees* (Psalm 37:35).

Why is that? Honestly, we don't have a very good answer (if we did, we would run for public office), except that it won't always be this way. Someday things are going to change dramatically—that's the subject of this chapter. For now, as long as you're living on this earth, things are *not* going to improve. We are *not* moving toward a better society, and we are *not* becoming better people. Just look around.

Some may argue that our technology is in the process of creating a better world. But for every new wonder drug developed in a lab, someone in another part of the world is figuring out how to make a more advanced destructive weapon. Some may tell you that our world is becoming more open-minded. But what that often means is that it's becoming more close-minded to the things of God. As people become more intolerant of the Christian perspective, they become more intolerant toward the people of God.

The Wicked Plot Against the Godly

As people put increasing faith in technology and human achievement, they usually turn farther away from God and make it increasingly difficult for Christians to express their faith publicly. There's a simple explanation for this. The world *hates* God and the world hates Jesus, who said this animosity arose because "I accuse it of sin and evil" (John 7:7).

Likewise, the world hates Christians, who are God's representatives on earth (John 15:19). Consequently, the world is doing everything it can to harass Christians and quiet their testimony. David knew this, and it frustrated him:

> *The wicked plot against the godly; they snarl at them in defiance* (Psalm 37:12).

We're Not Going to Win

Even if Christians do not go through the tribulation (and we hope we don't), it's going to get worse before it gets better. We can be an *influence* on society (Jesus calls us to be *salt* and *light*—Matthew 5:13,14), but we will not *change* society by beating back the forces of evil. To the contrary, we can expect to be beaten back. That's what Jesus meant when He said, "Since they persecuted me, naturally they will persecute you" (John 15:20).

Think about this for a moment. Jesus was opposed at every turn. As His followers, why should we have it any easier? Jesus was misunderstood at every word. Why should we expect people to fall down in wonder every time we open our mouths for God? Jesus was betrayed by someone He trusted. Why should we be surprised when friends turn against us?

Jesus was eventually deserted by His friends and killed by His enemies. You may not be in such mortal danger, but there's no guarantee. Each of Jesus' disciples except for one was put to death for his faith in Christ, and since that time millions of people have been martyred for their faith.

Why Didn't Jesus Call 10,000 Angels?

Good has not yet triumphed over evil for the same reason the Son of God was born on earth in obscurity, lived in humility, and died in apparent defeat: It was all part of God's plan.

When Jesus hung on that cross at Calvary, He could have called an army of angels to come and crush His opposition. He could have yanked Himself off that terrible cross and made Rambo look like a wimp by comparison. But He died, and He was buried. For a while it seemed as if sin and death had won. It seemed like the bad boys had crushed the good guys forever.

Then something happened—something so powerful and so significant that it shook the world and changed everything.

Jesus rose from the dead.

After three days, Jesus conquered death forever—and He did it for us. That's why we thank God, "who gives us victory over sin and death through Jesus Christ our Lord" (1 Corinthians 15:57).

This was all part of God's plan from the beginning.

> *God's secret plan has now been revealed to us; it is a plan centered on Christ, designed long ago according to his good pleasure. And this is his plan: At the right time he will bring everything together under the authority of Christ—everything in heaven and on earth* (Ephesians 1:9,10).

It's Only a Matter of Time

Although it may look like it sometimes, at no time in the history of the world has God ever lost control. Sin and the world are *not* out of control—not from God's perspective. He has a plan in place, and His plan is not yet finished. When we get upset at the apparent success of the wicked, "the Lord just laughs, for he sees their day of judgment" (Psalm 37:13).

Even when the tribulation hits full stride, with Satan and his superhuman allies marshaling the armies of the world against God and His chosen people (in what will surely be earth's darkest hour), the final chapter will not have been written.

Just when it seems that the victory of evil is assured, something so incredible and glorious will occur that the very foundation of the earth will shake. Just when the night is at its darkest hour, the dawn will break with ferocity and glory as the most

> *T*he testimony of faith is that, no matter how things look in this fallen world, all God's acts are wrought in perfect wisdom.
>
> —A. W. Tozer

anticipated event in human history finally arrives: the long-awaited second coming of Jesus Christ!

What Is the Second Coming?

The second coming of Christ is a future event in which Jesus Christ, the Son of God, will come from heaven to earth to finally and completely crush evil forever and introduce the future age and eternity. The second coming is such an important theme that it is mentioned 300 times in the New Testament alone.

"Is the Second Coming the Same as the Day of the Lord?"

The Greek word *parousia* is used in 2 Thessalonians 2:1 to describe the coming of Jesus to gather the believers:

> *And now, brothers and sisters, let us tell you about the coming again of our Lord Jesus Christ and how we will be gathered together to meet him.*

Later in the passage, "day of the Lord" is used to describe the return of Jesus to earth:

> *Please don't be so easily shaken and troubled by those who say that the day of the Lord has already begun. . . . For that day will not come until there is a great rebellion against God and the man of lawlessness is revealed—the one who brings destruction* (2 Thessalonians 2:2,3).

The End of the World According to Hollywood

The Postman. Nuclear war brings the world back to the nontechnological age. Most in the audience wished that this movie had never been delivered.

Many theologians point out that "coming" and "day of the Lord" are interchangeable, because later in the same passage, Paul uses "coming" (which in verse 1 seemed to describe the rapture) to describe the second coming:

> *Then the man of lawlessness will be revealed, whom the Lord Jesus will consume with the breath of his mouth and destroy by the splendor of his coming* (2 Thessalonians 2:8).

Some take the position, then, that the rapture and the second coming are the same event. This is the position of most amillennialists and some premillennialists.

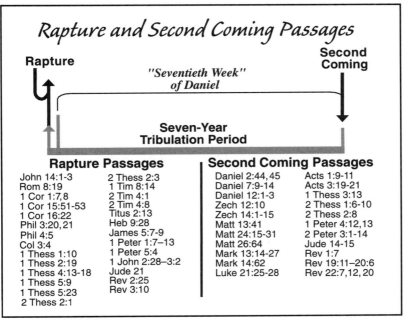

Rapture and Second Coming Passages

Rapture — "*Seventieth Week*" *of Daniel* — **Second Coming**

Seven-Year Tribulation Period

Rapture Passages		Second Coming Passages	
John 14:1-3	2 Thess 2:3	Daniel 2:44,45	Acts 1:9-11
Rom 8:19	1 Tim 8:14	Daniel 7:9-14	Acts 3:19-21
1 Cor 1:7,8	2 Tim 4:1	Daniel 12:1-3	1 Thess 3:13
1 Cor 15:51-53	2 Tim 4:8	Zech 12:10	2 Thess 1:6-10
1 Cor 16:22	Titus 2:13	Zech 14:1-15	2 Thess 2:8
Phil 3:20,21	Heb 9:28	Matt 13:41	1 Peter 4:12,13
Phil 4:5	James 5:7-9	Matt 24:15-31	2 Peter 3:1-14
Col 3:4	1 Peter 1:7–13	Matt 26:64	Jude 14-15
1 Thess 1:10	1 Peter 5:4	Mark 13:14-27	Rev 1:7
1 Thess 2:19	1 John 2:28–3:2	Mark 14:62	Rev 19:11–20:6
1 Thess 4:13-18	Jude 21	Luke 21:25-28	Rev 22:7,12, 20
1 Thess 5:9	Rev 2:25		
1 Thess 5:23	Rev 3:10		
2 Thess 2:1			

Thomas Ice and Timothy Demy

Rapture/Second Coming Contrasts

Rapture/Translation	Second Coming Established Kingdom
1. Translation of all believers	1. No translation at all
2. Translated saints go to heaven	2. Translated saints return to earth
3. Earth not judged	3. Earth judged and righteousness established
4. Imminent, any-moment, signless	4. Follows definite predicted signs, including tribulation
5. Not in the Old Testament	5. Predicted often in Old Testament
6. Believers only	6. Affects all humanity
7. Before the day of wrath	7. Concluding the day of wrath
8. No reference to Satan	8. Satan bound
9. Christ comes *for* His own	9. Christ comes *with* His own
10. He comes in the *air*	10. He comes to the *earth*
11. He claims His bride	11. He comes with His bride
12. Only His own see Him	12. Every eye shall see Him
13. Tribulation begins	13. Millennial kingdom begins

Courtesy of Thomas Ice and Timothy Demy

To review the previous chapters, we have talked about a series of events leading up to the second coming of Jesus:

✓ The world is going to get worse (2 Timothy 3:1).

✓ All Christians, both dead and living, will be caught up in the air to meet Jesus in the rapture (1 Thessalonians 4:15-18).

✓ The seven-year tribulation will unfold in two 3½-year segments (Daniel 9:27).

✓ Satan, the Antichrist, and the false prophet will mobilize their armies of human and demonic warriors in the greatest confrontation of good versus evil in the history of the world (Revelation 19:19-21).

Can you imagine the scene? Armageddon will be the most remarkable, frightening, and decisive battle in history. People who are alive at this moment in time will shake with sheer terror. But if you are one of those who was "caught up" with Jesus in the rapture before the second coming, you will experience something completely different. Are you ready for this?

You will be a real soldier in the "armies of heaven" following Jesus as He descends from heaven to earth to utterly crush the armies of hell.

Then I saw heaven opened, and a white horse was standing there. And the one sitting on the horse was named Faithful and True. For he judges fairly and then goes to war. His eyes were bright like flames of fire, and on his head were many crowns. A name was written on him, and only he knew what it meant. He was clothed with a robe dipped in blood, and his title was the Word of God. The armies of heaven, dressed in pure white linen, followed him on white horses. From his mouth came a sharp sword, and with it he struck down the nations. He ruled them with an iron rod, and he trod the winepress of the fierce wrath of almighty God. On his robe and thigh was written this title: King of kings and Lord of lords (Revelation 19:11-16).

There it is! The second coming of Jesus Christ. As if this description isn't enough to get your adrenalin pumping, the Bible provides us with several other characteristics of this glorious event.

The Nature of the Second Coming

Louis Berkhof, an expert on Bible prophecy, lists five characteristics of the second coming:

1. The second coming will be *personal*. After Jesus rose from the dead, He made several personal appearances to His disciples and hundreds of other people. Forty days after His bodily resurrection, Jesus "ascended" into heaven (Acts 1:9). As the disciples watched in wonder, an angel told them, "Jesus has been taken away from you into heaven. And someday, just as you saw him go, he will return!" (Acts 1:11). Just as Jesus left in person, He will return in person.

2. The second coming will be *physical*. Jesus will come to earth in His body, not in spirit (the way He comes now to those who receive Him as personal Savior). And everyone will see Him.

> Look! He comes with the clouds of heaven. And everyone will see him—even those who pierced him. And all the nations of the earth will weep because of him. Yes! Amen! (Revelation 1:7).

3. The second coming will be *visible*. Jesus will not be invisible. The whole world will see His coming, whether they want to or not.

> And when Christ, who is your real life, is revealed to the whole world, you will share in all his glory (Colossians 3:4).

4. The second coming will be *sudden*. You would think that after the events of the rapture, the tribulation, and Armageddon, people would be counting the days for the return of Christ. But the Bible tells us that people, deluded by the Antichrist and his cohorts, will be caught by surprise at His sudden return. The Scriptures are clear that once this happens, it will be *too late*.

> *I really don't need to write to you about how and when all this will happen, for you know quite well that the day of the Lord will come unexpectedly, like a thief in the night* (1 Thessalonians 5:1,2).

5. The second coming will be *glorious* and *triumphant*. When Jesus came to earth the first time, He came in humiliation and obscurity:

> *There was nothing beautiful or majestic about his appearance, nothing to attract us to him. He was despised and rejected—a man of sorrows, acquainted with bitterest grief. We turned our backs on him and looked the other way when he went by. He was despised, and we did not care* (Isaiah 53:2,3).

When He comes the second time, it will be a much different story. The return of Christ will be magnificent. He will be a mighty warrior, the conquering King, coming to earth with power and glory:

> *And then at last, the sign of the coming of the Son of Man will appear in the heavens, and there will be deep mourning among all the nations of the earth. And they will see the Son of Man arrive on the clouds of heaven with power and great glory* (Matthew 24:30).

Berkhof writes that when Jesus returns to earth—

- ✓ The clouds will be His chariot (Matthew 24:30)
- ✓ The angels, His bodyguard (2 Thessalonians 1:7)
- ✓ The archangels, his heralds (1 Thessalonians 4:16)
- ✓ The saints, "His glorious retinue" (1 Thessalonians 3:13)

The Purpose of the Second Coming

Is there more to the second coming than conquering the foes of God? Certainly, as Berkhof writes, "the destruction of all the evil forces that are hostile to God" is part of the reason for the second coming of Christ (2 Thessalonians 2:8). But there are other reasons to consider. Henry Thiessen lists seven:

1. To reveal Himself and His own. The people who lived when Jesus walked the earth had a distinct advantage over us. They could *see* Him! Ever since Jesus ascended to heaven, no one has seen Him. As a Christian, you now have the presence of Jesus in you (in the form of the Holy Spirit), but you can't actually see Him. All that will change when Jesus comes again. If you think having the Lord in your life now is amazing (and it is), you won't even be able to imagine what it will be like to actually *see* Him.

Yes, dear friends, we are already God's children, and we can't even imagine what we will be like when Christ returns. But we do know that when he comes we will be like him, for we will see him as he really is (1 John 3:2).

2. To judge the beast, the false prophet, and their armies. Jesus won't merely defeat His opponents. He will swiftly and completely judge and condemn them for all eternity:

> *Then I saw the beast gathering the kings of the earth and their armies in order to fight against the one sitting on the horse and his army. And the beast was captured, and with him the false prophet. . . . Both the beast and his false prophet were thrown alive into the lake of fire that burns with sulfur* (Revelation 19:19,20).

3. To bind Satan. Satan, God's mighty foe, will be captured and imprisoned for a thousand years:

> *Then I saw an angel come down from heaven with the key to the bottomless pit and a heavy chain in his hand. He seized the dragon—that old serpent, the Devil, Satan—and bound him in chains for a thousand years. The angel threw him into the bottomless pit, which he then shut and locked so Satan could not deceive the nations anymore until the thousand years were finished* (Revelation 20:1-3).

4. To save Israel. When Jesus came to earth the first time, He came for His people, the people of Israel. But they rejected Him as their Messiah (John 1:11). Does this mean that God has rejected Israel? The apostle Paul, himself a Jew, says, "No, God has not rejected his own people, whom he chose from the very beginning" (Romans 11:2). Paul explains that when Christ comes again, the Jews will finally accept Him:

Did God's people stumble and fall beyond recovery? Of course not! His purpose was to make his salvation available to the Gentiles, and then the Jews would be jealous and want it for themselves. Now if the Gentiles were enriched because the Jews turned down God's offer of salvation, think how much greater a blessing the world will share when the Jews finally accept it (Romans 11:11,12).

Chapter 9

5. To judge the nations. Thiessen suggest that after Christ has dealt with the Antichrist and his followers, He will gather all the nations before Him for judgment (for a complete treatment of the judgment, see chapter 9). Thiessen asserts that Scripture teaches that Jesus will judge the living nations on earth *before* the millennium (Matthew 25:31-46). All of the dead will be judged in the skies at the "great white throne" *after* the millennium (Revelation 20:11-15).

6. To deliver and bless creation. Can you imagine what kind of shape the earth will be in after the tribulation and Armageddon? God's glorious creation, which He pronounced as "good" at the beginning of the world (Genesis 1:25), will barely be inhabitable by the end of the world. One of the purposes for the second coming will be for Jesus to remove the curse of sin from the earth and restore creation to its original glory (Romans 8:19-22).

7. To set up His kingdom. Here is where we come to one of the most debated and interesting aspects of the end of the world: the kingdom of God. In the next

"What Is the Significance of David's Throne?"

King David, who established his throne in Jerusalem, played a very significant part in the life of Jesus, the King of kings. Jesus was a direct descendant of David (Matthew 1:6-16) and was born in the city of David (Luke 2:11). Someday, in the millennial kingdom, Jesus will rule from David's throne in Jerusalem (Luke 1:32).

It all goes back to the *covenant*—or promise—God made with David before he became king (2 Samuel 7:8-16). First of all, God promised that David would become Israel's greatest king. Second, God promised that He would raise up one of David's descendants and "establish the throne of his kingdom forever." Jesus was the fulfillment of this promise. He will reign in Jerusalem, and His kingdom will last forever.

section we're going to talk about one part of that kingdom, known as the *millennium*, but the kingdom of God is actually much larger. When Christ returns, one of His purposes will be to usher in the eternal kingdom. The Old Testament prophets wrote about this kingdom and the One who would rule it.

For a child is born to us, a son is given to us. And the government will rest on his shoulders. These will be

his royal titles: Wonderful Counselor, Mighty God,
Everlasting Father, Prince of Peace. His ever ex-
panding, peaceful government will never end. He
will rule forever with fairness and justice from the
throne of his ancestor David. The passionate commit-
ment of the LORD Almighty will guarantee this!
(Isaiah 9:6,7).

This famous passage of Scripture indicates that the
kingdom of God will include a literal rule of Jesus
Christ on the earth. He will sit on David's throne in
God's capital city, Jerusalem.

The Millennium: Fact or Fantasy?

In chapter 5 we talked about the various views of
Bible prophecy, which all center on the millennium.
We are going to proceed in this section with the *pre-*
millennial view, which treats the millennium as a literal, thousand-year end-of-the-world event. But you
need to keep in mind that some prominent Bible-
believing theologians (Berkhof, for example) believe
that there is no basis in Scripture for this understanding of the millennium. According to this *amillen-*
nial view, we are currently in the *spiritual* kingdom of
God, which will be followed immediately by the
eternal kingdom of God when Christ returns to earth.

Why Believe in a Literal Millennium?

With so much talk and hype about the millennium in
popular culture, it would be easy to trivialize the
biblical emphasis on the millennium. But believe us,

THE SPIRITUAL AND THE LITERAL KINGDOM OF GOD

Whatever your view on the millennium, it is important to recognize that the kingdom of God is *both* a *literal* and a *spiritual* kingdom. Jesus will literally rule during the millennium, and His rule will extend into eternity after the millennium. But there is a *spiritual* kingdom as well, which Alva J. McClain calls "that inner and therefore unseen rule of God over the hearts of men who yield themselves to His will." This is what Jesus meant when He said, "Make the Kingdom of God your primary concern" (Matthew 6:33). He was talking about letting God rule in your heart.

the attempts of the media pundits to make something important out of the year 2000 pale in comparison to the actual millennium that will someday exist on earth.

Millennium Fever

One of the reasons that ordinary people get millennium fever is because human beings have always dreamed about a future "golden age" on earth. Even people who reject the God of the Bible outright will often envision a future "utopia," a perfect world where all people will get along because human beings have finally evolved to near-perfection. Of course, an unrealistic view of man is at the center of such a fantasy world.

The Light of the Lord

One of the most consistent themes in the Bible is *light*. We love how this image flows through Scripture.

✓ God's first command was, "Let there be *light*" (Genesis 1:3).

✓ The prophets predicted that a *light* would come to people in darkness (Isaiah 9:2).

✓ Jesus came to earth to be that *light* (John 1:9).

✓ Those who reject Jesus love darkness more than *light* (John 3:19).

✓ Those who accept Jesus are the *light* of the world (Matthew 5:14).

✓ When Christ appears, His *light* will shine once again (2 Peter 1:19).

✓ In heaven there will be no sun, for the Son of God, who is the Sun of Righteousness (Malachi 4:2), will be all the *light* we need (Revelation 21:23).

The millennium spoken of in the Bible is the only true millennium, and it will be the kingdom of God, not the kingdom of man. Jesus Christ will rule, and His light will shine forth with such power that all who oppose Him will be consumed.

The LORD Almighty says, "The day of judgment is coming, burning like a furnace. The arrogant and the wicked will be burned up like straw on that day. They

will be consumed like a tree—roots and all. But for
you who fear my name, the Sun of Righteousness will
rise with healing in his wings. And you will go free,
leaping with joy like calves let out to pasture
(Malachi 4:1,2).

Here are some reasons why you can believe in a literal millennium on earth:

✓ A literal millennium fulfills the *promises of God,*
including the promise He made to *Abraham* that
his descendents would be a great nation in a literal land (Genesis 15:18-21); and to *David* that
his dynasty and kingdom would continue and
be secure forever (2 Samuel 7:16).

✓ A literal millennium fulfills the *purpose of Christ*
in coming back to earth to set up His kingdom
(Matthew 25:31).

✓ A literal millennium fulfills the *promise of*
Scripture that there will be a period during
which peace and righteousness will reign upon
the earth (Isaiah 2:4).

What Will the Millennium Be Like?

Thiessen offers seven characteristics of the literal
future millennium:

**1. Jesus Christ will personally rule from the
throne of David in Jerusalem.** Jesus will reign over
all the earth, bringing about a 1000-year period of
universal peace (Isaiah 2:4) and righteousness

(Jeremiah 23:5,6). He will keep things in order by swift judgment (Zechariah 14:17-19).

2. The church will reign with Christ. As the bride of Christ (Revelation 21:9), the church—which is made up of all believers—will reign with Christ over the Gentile world (2 Timothy 2:12).

3. Israel will be completely regathered and will recognize its King. All the people of Israel, God's chosen people, will be regathered and will become a great nation, just as God promised (Isaiah 11:10-13) and Jesus predicted (Matthew 24:30,31).

4. The nations of the earth will populate the millennium. Earlier in this chapter we pointed out that Jesus would judge the living before the millennium begins. These will be people who have survived the tribulation. Jesus prophesied that He would separate "the sheep from the goats" (Matthew 25:31-34). The sheep will evidently be those who accepted Christ during the tribulation, and the goats those who rejected Him. Thiessen says that these sheep will be a part of the millennial kingdom and "will form the nucleus of the kingdom, together with the restored and converted Israel."

Together, the Gentile nations and the restored nation of Israel will go up to Jerusalem to worship the King (Isaiah 2:2-4).

5. Satan will be out of the picture during the millennium. The Bible is very clear that Satan will be captured, bound, and thrown into the bottomless pit

---

GLAD YOU ASKED *"Will People Be Born and Die During the Millennium?"*

The Bible is clear that the millennium will be an incredible time to live. People will not only be born, but they will live much longer than they do now. In fact, only "sinners" will die as "young" as 100 years old (Isaiah 65:20). Thiessen says that people born during this time will need to be "evangelized" (that is, hear the good news about Jesus), and Israel will be the evangelists (Isaiah 66:19).

---

during the millennium (Revelation 20:1-3). We have no idea what that will mean to the world, since we have only known a world where Satan rules. With Jesus in charge and Satan enchained (along with his legions of demons), life during the millennium will be glorious. And while people will still have the ability to sin, the temptation to sin will be virtually nonexistent.

6. Nature will be restored to near-perfection. The presence of sin and Satan in our world today does more than corrupt people. It also affects nature. Nature itself has been "groaning as in the pains of childbirth right up to the present time" (Romans 8:22). When Christ reigns on earth, nature will be delivered from that curse.

*All creation anticipates the day when it will join
God's children in glorious freedom from death and
decay* (Romans 8:21).

Think of it! Nature will finally do what it was created
to do: exist in harmony and perfect balance. There
won't be any earthquakes, hurricanes, volcanic erup-
tions, or forest fires. We think there probably won't be
the need for Round-Up (because there won't be any
weeds) or sunscreen (because there won't be any
harmful radiation).

7. In general, conditions will be heavenly. The millennium will be as close to "heaven on earth" as possible—but it won't be heaven (for that you'll have to
wait for chapter 10). With Jesus as their ruler, people
will have direct access to the all-powerful, all-
knowing, and all-loving God.

*For my people will live as long as trees and will have
time to enjoy their hard-won gains. They will not
work in vain, and their children will not be doomed to
misfortune. For they are people blessed by the* LORD,
*and their children, too, will be blessed. I will answer
them before they even call to me. While they are still
talking to me about their needs, I will go ahead and
answer their prayers! The wolf and lamb will feed together. The lion will eat straw like the ox. Poisonous
snakes will strike no more. In those days, no one will
be hurt or destroyed on my holy mountain. I, the*
LORD, *have spoken!* (Isaiah 65:22-25).

What Will Happen When the Millennium Ends?

If there's one thing you can say about Satan (and we're not talking about an admirable quality here—it's more like stupidity), it's that he doesn't know when he's defeated. The Bible says that at the conclusion of the millennium, Satan will be let out of his prison. Fool that he is, he will try to mount yet another rebellion against God and His people (Revelation 20:7,8). This will literally be his last gasp. As you'll see in the next chapter, Satan will be crushed, defeated, judged, and sentenced forever.

After the brief rebellion of Satan, "the whole world has now become the kingdom of our Lord and of his Christ, and he will reign forever and ever" (Revelation 11:15).

What Does All This Mean to You?

The second coming of Jesus Christ to earth will be the most magnificent event the world has ever known. If you have accepted Jesus as your personal Savior—or you make that decision before the rapture—then you will have a front-row seat as Jesus returns to earth at the end of the world. More than that, you will have a place of honor and prominence as you rule in the millennial kingdom with the King of kings and Lord of lords.

But what difference does all of this future talk mean to you now? Here's what we think.

The anticipation of the return of Christ to earth in the *future* should encourage you to live for Christ on earth *now* as you remember what He did for you in the *past*.

This is what William Hendriksen calls "living in three tenses." The Christian is the only person capable of living this way—

✓ Understanding what Jesus did for us in the *past* to secure our future.

> *Now we live with a wonderful expectation because Jesus Christ rose again from the dead. For God has reserved a priceless inheritance for his children. It is kept in heaven for you, pure and undefiled, beyond the reach of change and decay. And God, in his mighty power, will protect you until you receive this salvation, because you are trusting him. It will be revealed on the last day for all to see* (1 Peter 1:3-5).

✓ Realizing that our *present* troubles are only temporary.

> *And even we Christians, although we have the Holy Spirit within us as a foretaste of future glory, also groan to be released from pain and suffering. We, too, wait anxiously for that day when God will give us our full rights as his children, including the new bodies he has promised us* (Romans 8:23).

✓ Anticipating that Jesus is coming in the *future*, even though we don't know when that will be.

> *The Lord isn't really being slow about his promise to return, as some people think. No, he is being patient for your sake. He does not want anyone to perish, so he is giving more time for everyone to repent. But the day of the Lord will come as unexpectedly as a thief* (2 Peter 3:9,10).

"What's That Again?"

1. While we're on this earth, we are going to *influence*, not change society.

2. It's only a matter of time before Jesus returns to set things right.

3. When Jesus returns to earth to set up His Kingdom, He will do it in a way that is *personal, physical, visible, sudden,* and *glorious.*

4. Jesus will establish His kingdom on earth during the millennium, which is a literal period of a thousand years following the second coming.

5. After the millennium, Jesus will crush Satan for good and usher in His eternal kingdom.

6. As you anticipate the return of Christ in the *future*, you should live for Christ *now* on earth as you remember what Jesus did for you in the *past*.

Dig Deeper

All About the Second Coming by Herbert Lockyer. Dr. Lockyer is known for his "All About" books on the Bible. In this book he takes what the Bible says about the second coming of Christ at "face value."

The Bible on the Hereafter by William Hendriksen. This amillennial approach to the second coming provides a good balance to the premillennial books on the same subject.

The Revelation of Jesus Christ by John Walvoord. Our premillennial friend has a good chapter on the second coming in this commentary on the Book of Revelation.

Four Views on the Book of Revelation edited by C. Marvin Pate. The four major views on interpreting Revelation are presented by four Bible scholars. The presentation of each view is then followed by a response from a different perspective.

The Greatness of the Kingdom by Alva J. McClain. A classic book on the kingdom of God, including the universal, spiritual, and literal aspects of the kingdom.

Moving On . . .

We told you at the beginning of Part III that there would be a lot of "good news/bad news" information in our discussion of the end times. The second coming of Jesus Christ will be *very* good news for many, but for everyone else the news will be extremely bad. It would be very comforting to imagine that after all the events we've talked about in Part III, God is going to turn into a softie and say, "Hey, I'm in a good mood, so everybody makes it!"

As silly as that seems, that's the way a lot of people think. You've certainly heard someone make the statement that "a loving God would never send anyone to hell." They're hoping against hope that God is going to open the doors of heaven and let everyone in. Well, He's going to open the doors of heaven all right (read all about it in chapter 10), but first there's this little matter of judgment. As sure as you're reading this book, it's going to happen. And it's the subject of our next chapter.

**Chapter
10**

Chapter 9

Judgment Day:
Here Comes the Judge

I n today's society, the concept of hell is going out of style. But it is certainly not going out of business.

—*Unknown*

If you are reading this chapter, you are to be congratulated. Most people would rather skip the subject of death and dying. They want to avoid it at all costs, pretending (and desperately hoping) that they won't ever die. But in the event they do kick the proverbial bucket, they hope that what follows death is nothing more scary than harps, halos, and a few hallelujahs.

Well, according to the Bible, after death you are either going to get "bad news" (actually, *horrible* news) or "good news" (actually, *tremendous* news). You see, your final destination is going to be determined by whether you accepted or rejected Jesus Christ during your lifetime. The final destinations are so opposite, that we are going to treat them in different chapters. After we talk about death and judgment in this chapter, we'll conclude with a discussion of hell (the final destination for those who reject Christ). Chapter 10 is devoted to the subject of heaven (the final destination of those who accept Christ).

Just so you don't get depressed reading about death, here is our helpful hint for reading chapter 9: Hell is optional. That's right! You don't have to go there if you don't want to. We'll explain more later, but we want you to know going into this chapter that your future doesn't have to include doom and gloom. The "good news" or "bad news" in your future is all a matter of choice—and as you'll see in this chapter, it's a helluva choice (pun *intended*).

Bruce & Stan

Chapter 9

Judgment Day:
Here Comes the Judge

What's Ahead

- ➤ Death: the final frontier
- ➤ Standing before the judge
- ➤ The forgiven at the judgment seat of Christ: rewards only
- ➤ The guilty at the great white throne judgment: dead men walking
- ➤ Hell: the forever home of the condemned
- ➤ So what does all this mean to you?

Nobody wants to do it, but everybody does. No, we aren't talking about paying taxes, going to the dentist, or reading the tabloid headlines while standing in the checkout line at the grocery store. We're talking about death. There! We said it. Now it's out in the open.

In this chapter we are going to talk about death, and judgment too. No one can escape them. Okay, if you read chapter 6, you know that the Christians who are living at the time of the rapture will be swooshed off the earth without dying. But except for that select group, everyone else will experience death. And everyone from all time (even the rapture riders) will stand before God for a time of final judgment.

The Word No One Ever Wants to Say

I am a lawyer, and I specialize in estate planning and probate: wills, trusts, and ways for people to pass their wealth to the next generation (either during life or at death). To put it bluntly, I am a specialist in planning for transfers of wealth by "gifts and stiffs."

I have noticed that people do not even want to use the word *death*. Perhaps it has too much stark reality to it. So they use euphemisms for death and dying. Here are some of my favorites, listed by category:

Traditional

- Pass away
- Pass on
- Expire
- Go to eternal rest

Contemporary

- Keel over
- Croak
- Kick the bucket
- Bite the big burrito

Destinational

- Pass over
  (. . . to the other side)
- Go to the
  Great Beyond
- Go six feet under

Behavioral

- Meet my Maker
- Pull the final curtain
- Push up the daisies

Death: the Final Frontier

All these years, Captain Kirk and the other commanders of the starship Enterprise have been wrong. Space is *not* the final frontier. Let's face it: We know a lot more about space than we know about what happens when we die. And while everyone who has ever lived has died, no one has come back to tell us what it's like. So for those of us who have yet to make the journey, *death* is the final frontier.

What Is Death?

The answer to this question may not be as simple as you think. Anyone older than a toddler can understand the concept of *physical* death, but there is more to it than that. Here are a few biblical insights on life and death.

✓ Physical death is undeniable and inevitable.

> *There is a time for everything. . . . A time to be born and a time to die. . . . The same destiny ultimately awaits everyone, whether they are righteous or wicked, good or bad* (Ecclesiastes 3:1,2; 9:2).

> *It is destined that each person dies only once and after that comes judgment* (Hebrews 9:27).

I hate death. In fact, I could live forever without it.

—Pogo

*I*t's not that I'm afraid to die. I just don't want to be there when it happens.

—Woody Allen

✓ Your spirit lives on after your body dies.

> *Don't be afraid of those who want to kill you. They can only kill your body; they cannot touch your soul* (Matthew 10:28).

✓ Sometimes when the Bible talks about death, it is referring to spiritual (or eternal) death. Even though your spirit is immortal and will live forever, spiritual death means that your soul will be eternally separated from God.

> *For the wages of sin is death* (Romans 6:23).

✓ Conversely, when the Bible talks about eternal life, it is referring to your spirit living in the presence of God.

> *. . . but the free gift of God is eternal life through Christ Jesus our Lord* (Romans 6:23).

One of our favorite Bible scholars, Millard J. Erickson, made this comment: "Life and death, according to Scripture, are not to be thought of as existence and nonexistence, but as two different states of existence. Death is simply a transition to a different mode of existence; it is not, as some tend to think, extinction."

Where Do I Go When I Die?

Gee, how many bazillion people have asked that question before? Just about everyone who has ever lived. The answer depends upon whether you accepted or rejected Christ during your lifetime.

Jesus Answers the Question with a Story

So you want to know where you go immediately after you die? Well, Jesus answered this question with a story of the beggar and a rich man.

> *There was a certain rich man who was splendidly clothed and who lived each day in luxury. At his door lay a diseased beggar named Lazarus. . . . The beggar died and was carried by the angels to be with Abraham. The rich man also died and was buried, and his soul went to the place of the dead. There, in torment, he saw Lazarus in the far distance with Abraham. The rich man shouted, "Father Abraham, have some pity! Send Lazarus over here to dip the tip of his finger in water and cool my tongue, because I am in anguish in these flames." But Abraham said to him, "Son, remember that during your lifetime you had everything you wanted, and Lazarus had nothing. So now he is here being comforted, and you are in anguish. And besides, there is a great chasm separating us. Anyone who wanted to cross over to you from here is stopped at its edge, and no one there can cross over to us"* (Luke 16:19-26).

Here is what we can learn from this story:

✓ There is a separation between these two places which cannot be crossed.
✓ Once you are in one place, you can't go to the other. There is no changing your mind after death.
✓ Lazarus was in complete comfort.
✓ The rich man was in agony.

"What About Purgatory?"

Purgatory is primarily a Roman Catholic teaching. It is a "half-way" place for those who aren't bad enough to go directly to hades and hell, and those who aren't yet good enough to go directly to heaven. This teaching says that those on earth can help move the inhabitants of purgatory toward heaven by means of Mass, prayers, and good works.

Protestantism rejects this Catholic teaching for two major reasons. First, it is based primarily on ancient writings (which were mostly written between the Old and New Testaments) which Protestants do not accept as canonical Scripture. Second, the teaching implies that salvation can be earned through doing deeds, which is completely contrary to the New Testament teaching that salvation is a free gift of God's grace. More on this in chapter 11.

✓ For *non-Christians: It's off to hades . . . judgment's waiting room.* In the "intermediate state" between physical death and judgment, the unbelievers are in a type of waiting room (but time there is much worse than reading outdated magazines in the doctor's office). The Old Testament Hebrew word for this place is *sheol* and the Greek word in the New Testament is *hades.*

✓ *For Christians: on to heaven—no waiting.* In sharp contrast, Christians who die will go directly to the presence of the Lord. There is no probation, no waiting room. (They will have a time of judgment to follow, but it will be a time of passing out rewards).

What Is the Effect of Physical Death?

For the non-Christian, there is nothing positive about death. It marks the irreversible beginning of eternal torment, starting in hades, and then getting unbelievably worse in hell (after the judgment). But for the Christian, death is not something to be feared. In fact, the apostle Paul said that he looked forward to death because it meant being with Christ:

> *For to me, living is for Christ, and dying is even better. Yet if I live, that means fruitful service for Christ. I really don't know which is better. I'm torn between two desires: Sometimes I want to live, and sometimes I long to go and be with Christ* (Philippians 1:21-23).

Standing Before the Judge

Make no mistake about it: A time of final judgment is coming. This is the clear teaching of the Old Testament:

> *God will judge us for everything we do, including every secret thing, whether good or bad* (Ecclesiastes 12:14).

"Why Is Judgment Necessary?"

GLAD YOU ASKED God doesn't need a court proceeding to determine what we have done in life. He already knows that. His judgment is to impose the death penalty for sin for those who did not accept Christ's forgiveness (Romans 6:23), *or* to reward those who have been forgiven for their service to God (Matthew 25:14-30).

And the New Testament:

> *The day will surely come when God, by Jesus Christ, will judge everyone's secret life* (Romans 2:16).

There is an old joke about the governor who walked through the penitentiary, talking to each of the prisoners. He finally came to one convict who admitted that he was guilty of a crime. The governor immediately pardoned the convict with this explanation: "All of the other prisoners said that they were innocent. I had to release him before he corrupted the others."

When the time of final judgment comes, we don't think that anyone is going to be screaming that they are innocent. They will come face-to-face with a perfect judge.

Who Is the Judge?

While God is the judge of all (Hebrews 12:23), He has delegated this task to His Son, Jesus Christ:

The Father leaves all judgment to his Son, so that everyone will honor the Son, just as they honor the Father (John 5:22,23).

Christ will be judging all people from all nations and from all ages of history.

Sheep on the Right; Goats on the Left

In Matthew 25, Jesus described the judgment scene:

- ✓ He will be sitting on a throne in all His glory, with His angels around Him.
- ✓ All the people of all nations will be gathered in His presence.
- ✓ Like a shepherd, He will separate the "sheep" from the "goats."
- ✓ The "sheep"—all the people who accepted Him—will go to His right side.
- ✓ The "goats"—all those who rejected Him—will go to His left side.
- ✓ The "sheep" are welcomed into the kingdom of God.
- ✓ The "goats" are sent to eternal punishment with Satan and the demons.

The Who and the When

Throughout history, God has imposed judgments at different times and occasions.

The End of the World According to Hollywood

The Andromeda Strain has the world's population on the brink of extermination when a satellite reenters the earth's atmosphere carrying a deadly bacteria. Fortunately for the world, the virus is put to sleep by this movie's boring cast.

✓ The great flood in Noah's day was God's judgment upon evil humanity (Genesis 6–8).

✓ The Jews wandering in the wilderness for 40 years was God's judgment imposed for their lack of faith (Numbers 14).

✓ Ananias and Sapphira were struck dead by God as immediate judgment for their lying (Acts 5).

But these were individual, isolated judgments by God. They can be contrasted with the "final judgment," which will occur at the end of the tribulation when Christ comes again. At that time, everyone will be judged (and there will be no escaping it).

> *Look, the Lord is coming with thousands of his holy ones. He will bring the people of the world to judgment. He will convict the ungodly of all the evil things they have done in rebellion and of all the insults godless sinners have spoken against him* (Jude 14,15).

But everyone will not be judged at the same time, and all the judgments will not have the same result.

✓ *Judgment of the Antichrist and the false prophet.* At the end of the battle of Armageddon, the hordes of the world's armies will turn against the coming Christ. But Christ will slay them all, and He will take the Antichrist (the "beast") and the false prophet and cast them into hell (the "lake of fire"), where they will spend eternity (Revelation 19:19,20).

✓ *Judgment of Satan and his demons.* At the second coming, Satan will be bound by Christ and cast into an abyss for 1000 years. At the end of the millennium, Satan will be let loose for a short time, and he'll try to gather an army to battle Christians at the city of Jerusalem. But God will intervene by pouring fire from the sky. Satan will be captured, judged, and cast into the lake of fire (which will be the same fate for his demons).

> But fire from heaven came down on the attacking armies and consumed them. Then the Devil, who betrayed them, was thrown into the lake of fire that burns with sulfur, joining the beast and the false prophet. There they will be tormented day and night forever and ever (Revelation 20:9,10).

✓ *Judgment of believers.* Christians don't escape judgment just because they have accepted Christ as their Savior. But their judgment will be completely different than the judgment for unbelievers. After the rapture, Christians will stand before "the judgment seat of Christ" (explained on next page).

✓ *Judgment of unbelievers.* At the end of the millennium, all the people from all of history who failed to believe in Christ will be resurrected for their final judgment. This judgment is known as "the great white throne judgment" and is discussed on page 253.

"What About the People Who Lived Before Jesus?"

How is God going to judge those who lived and died before Jesus' death on the cross? How can they be expected to have a saving belief in Christ when He wasn't even around while they were living? Good questions.

For those who lived during Old Testament times, God will examine their faith in Him. The question is not whether they believed in Jesus, but whether they had faith in God. If they did, then the work of Jesus on the cross covers their sins. The best example may be Abraham. Of his faith in God, the Bible says:

> *And Abram believed the LORD, and the LORD declared him righteous because of his faith* (Genesis 15:6).

The Forgiven at the Judgment Seat of Christ: Rewards Only

Great news for Christians! Their judgment is not going to involve any penalties. Sure, they did stuff wrong during their lifetime—lots of stuff. But by accepting Jesus Christ as their Savior, all of their sins (past, present, and future) are forgiven. So they are declared "not guilty."

So now there is no condemnation for those who be-long to Christ Jesus (Romans 8:1).

The judgment of Christians is called "the judgment seat of Christ." The Greek word used by Paul for "judgment seat" is *bema*. The *bema* was the judge's bench at the Olympic stadium in ancient Corinth in Greece. When an athlete won the race, he would step up onto the *bema* to receive his award. Because of this, the judgment day for Christians is called the "bema seat" judgment.

Jewels or Junk

The judgment seat of Christ will *not* be an examina-tion of Christians' sins. But it will be an examination of the quality of their service to God. In other words, how well did they handle the gifts, talents, resources, and opportunities which God gave to each of them? The apostle Paul explained the nature of this judg-ment by using a word picture from the building trade. In his illustration, the "foundation" is solid because it represents salvation in Jesus Christ. But the building inspector (Christ) is going to inspect the quality of the building materials for what was con-structed on that foundation.

> *But whoever is building on this foundation must be very careful. For no one can lay any other foundation than the one we already have—Jesus Christ. Now anyone who builds on that foundation may use gold, silver, jewels, wood, hay, or straw. But there is going to come a time of testing at the judgment day to see*

*what kind of work each builder has done.
Everyone's work will be put through the fire to see
whether or not it keeps its value. If the work sur-
vives the fire, that builder will receive a reward.
But if the work is burned up, the builder will suffer
great loss. The builders themselves will be saved,
but like someone escaping through a wall of flames*
(1 Corinthians 3:10-15).

Here is what we can learn from Paul's illustration
about the judgment seat of Christ:

✓ Some of the things we do for Christ are valuable
(like gold, silver, and jewels). These count for
something, and will entitle us to some kind of
reward.

✓ Other things we do on earth are a waste of time
as far as God is concerned. We may be acting
religious, but if God isn't pleased by what we
are doing, then our actions are as worthless as
building with wood, hay, and straw. There is no
reward for such junk.

Jesus also told some parables which indicate the
question which Jesus will be asking at the judgment
seat of Christ: "What have you done with what I
have given you?" The parable of the ten servants
(Luke 19:11-27) shows that not everyone gets the
same opportunities or resources. Christians won't be
competing against each other at this judgment, but
they will be held responsible for how well they managed what God gave to them.

"Let's Tell Our Contestants What They Have Won!"

No one knows for sure what kind of "rewards" the faithful Christian will receive at the judgment seat of Christ. It probably won't be money or things of a material nature since that kind of stuff will be meaningless in heaven (and we surely won't even be interested in it when we are in the presence of God). Many commentators believe that the "rewards" will be some type of privileged service to God, such as ruling in a position of authority during the millennium.

The Guilty at the Great White Throne Judgment: Dead Men Walking

In the Book of Revelation, John describes the judgment day that all unbelievers will face:

And I saw a great white throne, and I saw the one who was sitting on it. The earth and sky fled from his presence, but they found no place to hide. I saw the dead, both great and small, standing before God's throne. And the books were opened, including the Book of Life. And the dead were judged according to the things written in the books, according to what they had done. . . . And anyone whose name was not found recorded in the Book of Life was thrown into the lake of fire (Revelation 20:11-15).

This "great white throne judgment" is for all people who have rejected God's plan of salvation. There is no question about their guilt. Their sin has made them guilty:

> *There is no judgment awaiting those who trust him. But those who do not trust him have already been judged for not believing in the only Son of God* (John 3:18).

God knows those who belong to Him. Their names are written in "the Book of Life" (Luke 10:20; Revelation 3:5). At this judgment, the Book of Life will be opened, and the names of the unbelievers will be found nowhere in the book. Christ Himself will say: "I don't know you. Go away" (Luke 13:27), and they will join Satan, the Antichrist, and the false prophet in the lake of fire.

Hell: the Forever Home of the Condemned

Have you been wondering about the "lake of fire" that we've been discussing? Well, wonder no more. That is Bible terminology for "hell." This is the place to which the unbelievers are sentenced following the great white throne judgment. We can learn about hell by looking at how the Bible describes it (or the condition of its inhabitants):

- ✓ outer darkness (Matthew 8:12)
- ✓ furnace (Matthew 13:42)
- ✓ weeping and gnashing of teeth (Matthew 13:42)

✓ eternal fire (Matthew 25:41)

✓ eternal punishment (Matthew 25:46)

✓ terrible punishment (Romans 2:5)

✓ everlasting destruction (2 Thessalonians 1:9)

✓ bottomless pit (Revelation 9:1,2)

✓ tormented with fire and burning sulfur (Revelation 14:10,11)

✓ the lake that burns with fire and sulfur (Revelation 21:8)

✓ the second death (Revelation 21:8)

One Thing You Gotta Know for Sure

The most defining characteristic of hell, however, will not be the "gnashing of teeth" (although you don't see *that* too often). It will be the absence of the presence of God:

> . . . *forever separated from the Lord and from his glorious power (2 Thessalonians 1:9).*

This is what makes hell the complete opposite of heaven.

And There's More Bad News

There are two other features about hell which make it such a dreaded place: its finality and its eternality.

When you speak of heaven, let your face light up, let it glow with a heavenly gleam, let your eyes shine with His reflected glory. But when you speak of hell—well, then your ordinary face will do.

—Charles H. Spurgeon

> ### "Can God Really Sentence People to Hell?"
>
> **GLAD YOU ASKED**
>
> We can see how you might wonder about this if you perceive God to be just a kindly, old, lenient, and permissive grandfather-type. Couldn't He just "look the other way" with a "humans will be humans" attitude? Well, He can't—because He is God.
>
> Now don't get the idea that He is a mean old tyrant. Just the opposite. He is a loving God, and He does not want any of us to go to hell. But He is also a righteous and holy God, and He cannot let sin go unpunished.

Finality. When the verdict is imposed at the great white throne judgment, there will be no second chance. It's final. While some people dispute this view (and you can understand why they might want to believe that a second chance is possible), there is not a single verse in the Bible which indicates that anyone will have an opportunity for changing his or her belief after the final judgment. In fact, the verses you can read actually reinforce the finality of it all.

✓ "Away with you, you cursed ones, into the eternal fire prepared for the Devil and his demons!" (Matthew 25:41).

"Do You Suppose the Suffering of Hell Could Just Be Symbolic?"

Some critics say that the biblical references to hell are merely metaphorical, meaning that it is not real but simply symbolic. We (and most outstanding Bible scholars) have a hard time swallowing that notion. There are just too many specific references to hell as an actual place, with detailed descriptions of the suffering that is going to occur there. Hell will not just be a symbolic separation from God. There will be actual agony and torment for all of its inhabitants.

✓ And the story which Jesus told about Lazarus shows that the rich man wanted to change things but couldn't (see Luke 16:19-31).

Eternality. An unbeliever's sentence to hell is not only irreversible, it is also one that lasts forever. It is a death sentence which doesn't end with death, because you never die. Instead, you suffer for eternity. There is a minority viewpoint, annihilationism, which says that the inhabitants of hell will eventually burn up and be annihilated. We can't square this viewpoint with the many verses which describe hell with words like *everlasting, eternal,* or *forever and ever.* It seems clear that it will be a never-ending torture.

So What Does All This Mean To You?

Let's review what we know:

- ✓ Everybody dies, and there will eventually be a judgment for everyone.

- ✓ Believers will be at the judgment seat of Christ because of what *He* has done, and they go to heaven.

- ✓ Unbelievers will be at the great white throne judgment because of what *they* have done, and they go to hell.

- ✓ Hell is a place of unbelievable agony, and it never ends. (We don't talk about heaven until the next chapter, but you gotta know that it is better than hell!)

Think about what all of this means. It you want to avoid hell, then you have to avoid the great white throne judgment. If you want to avoid that judgment, then you need to respond to Jesus Christ.

You see, as we pointed out in the introduction to this chapter, hell is a choice. It certainly isn't God's plan for you. He doesn't want you to perish (2 Peter 3:9). In fact, God wants everyone to be saved and to understand the truth (1 Timothy 2:4).

C. S. Lewis was an atheist who tried to prove that God didn't exist. In the process of doing so, he became convinced of exactly the opposite and became one of Christianity's boldest defenders. In clarifying his view that hell is a choice, Lewis said this "Sin is a person's saying to God throughout life, 'Go away and leave me alone.' Hell is God's finally saying to that individual, 'You may have your wish.'"

Hell isn't something that God does *to* us. It is something that we *deserve* because of our sin. But we always have the option of obtaining forgiveness for our sins if we will submit our lives to Jesus. The choice is ours.

"What's That Again?"

1. Death comes to everyone (unless you are raptured). We will all experience a physical, bodily death, but we all have a spirit (soul) which lives forever.

2. A final judgment awaits everyone after death. For Christians, it will happen after the rapture. For unbelievers, it will occur after the millennium.

3. The judgment for believers is known as the judgment seat of Christ. They are not judged for their sins, because their sins were forgiven when they believed in Jesus Christ.

4. Unbelievers will go through the great white throne judgment. The verdict is a foregone conclusion, because each of them is guilty of sin. The penalty for this unforgiven sin is eternal banishment from the presence of God. Hell is not a fantasy; it is a real place with everlasting suffering and torment.

Dig Deeper

There is no shortage of books on the subjects of death, judgment, and hell. Here are three that you might find interesting if you want to look further at these issues:

Four Views of Hell edited by William Crocket. Four leading scholars each present their own viewpoint, representing the literal, metaphorical, purgatorial, and conditional positions. In an interesting "counterpoint," they take turns interacting with each other's positions.

The Last Days Handbook by Robert Lightner. There is a helpful question-and-answer format right at the beginning of Lightner's book which addresses death and judgment issues. But this book has much more than that alone. It has good overall coverage of all the end-times issues.

End Times by John Walvoord. This book is a collection of Dr. Walvoord's best writings on prophecy. Pay special attention to his chapter on rewards and judgment.

Systematic Theology by Wayne Grudem. This sturdy volume is a valuable resource for studying the whole spectrum of theology. Chapter 56 contains a particularly meaty discussion of issues related to hell and judgment.

Moody Handbook of Theology by Paul Enns. A much easier book to read than Grudem's, but still very thorough in its presentation of important theological issues. It contains lots of helpful Biblical insights into the questions of hell and judgment.

Moving On . . .

You've just read about the horrors of hell. Now it is time to read about the hope of heaven. Just as there is nothing in our experience that allows us to accurately imagine how bad hell is, we have no ability to comprehend the wonders of heaven. But don't let that stop you from reading. What you can read and understand will be amazing enough.

Chapter 10

Heaven:
Our Greatest Hope

I f I find in myself a desire which no experience in this world can satisfy, the most probable explanation is that I was made for another world.

—*C. S. Lewis*

Time magazine recently featured a story about heaven. The cover was a picture of a man standing on a cloud in a bright blue sky. The headline read, "Does Heaven Exist?"

What about you? Do you think heaven exists? Do you think heaven is a real place where people go when they die? Who goes there? What will they do? We ask these questions because heaven has always been a mystery to us. Even the apostle Paul couldn't find the words to describe heaven:

> *No eye has seen, no ear has heard, and no mind has imagined what God has prepared for those who love him* (1 Corinthians 2:9).

Heaven is hard to imagine because it is far beyond even our wildest dreams. Yet that shouldn't deter us from *trying* to imagine it, and it shouldn't stop us from *longing* for heaven. Because heaven is our greatest hope.

Bruce & Stan

Chapter 10

Heaven:
Our Greatest Hope

The chapters you have just read—about the rapture, the tribulation, the second coming, and judgment—have been pretty intense. If you've read them in order, you're probably ready for a refreshing change, like a scoop of sherbet after a heavy meal of meat and potatoes.

Perhaps you've been reading this book from the beginning and are hoping that at some point there will be a payoff. You want very much for us to tell you about the big reward. Or you may have turned to this chapter first because you want to learn more about a subject that has fascinated people since the beginning of time. You've got questions that no one has been able to answer.

Once again, it's Bruce and Stan to the rescue! We think we can help you by answering most of your questions in this chapter. So sit back in your favorite

┌───┐
│   │
│   *Survey Said*   │
│   │
│   When *Time* magazine did a survey for their cover story │
│   on heaven, they asked, "Do you believe in the existence │
│   of heaven, where people live forever with God after they │
│   die?" More than eight out of ten adults who responded │
│   said "yes."   │
│   │
└───┘

chair and get ready to open your heart and your
mind to the greatest subject—next to God Himself—
that you will ever think about, dream about, and
hope for: heaven.

The Hope of Heaven

As long as you're comfortable, let your mind drift for
a moment. Think back to when you were a kid. Did
you ever lie back on a grassy hillside and wonder,
"What's out there?" Whether you were looking at the
clouds or the stars, you probably wondered if "out
there" included heaven.

Did you ever ask your parents about heaven? Have
your kids ever asked you? Probably so, because next
to the question, "Is there a God?" the question we
mortals most frequently ask is, "Does heaven exist?"

One of the reasons for this response is surely that
God has "planted eternity in the human heart" (Ecclesiastes 3:11). But the other great reason concerns
hope.

"But I'm Happy Now!"

"I'm happy with my life," you might say. "I love the beauty of God's creation, I love my family, I love my job, and I love ice cream. I'm a happy camper. What more could I possibly want?"

Fantastic! We're not here to say that it's necessary to be miserable for you to long for heaven. But even the most fulfilled people on earth eventually come to realize that ultimate satisfaction can only be found in someone and something beyond ourselves. That *someone* is God, and that *something* is heaven.

Because we live in an imperfect world—full of disease, war, and natural disasters (and that's just in your family)—we live with the *hope* that *somewhere* there is a better place, free from the uncertainty and pain of this world. Because we toil and work and worry all our days, we *hope* that *someday* our stress and concerns and negative emotions will be put to rest, replaced with true happiness and everlasting contentment.

In other words, we are hoping for heaven.

And even we Christians, although we have the Holy Spirit within us as a foretaste of future glory, also groan to be released from pain and suffering. We, too, wait anxiously for that day when God will give us our full rights as his children (Romans 8:23).

What Will Heaven Be Like?

Trying to describe heaven may be the most difficult thing we will do in this book. We have gone to the Scriptures and done our best to tell you what heaven will be like, but we have also consulted with many experts who know more about heaven that we ever will (in other words, we've read a lot of books about heaven, which are listed at the end of this chapter). Because, though the Bible is very specific about the fact that there *is* a heaven, it doesn't go into a lot of detail about what it will be like to be there.

A Short Description

Heaven is a real *place*, created by God, that will exist forever. Heaven is where Jesus lives now (Acts 3:21) and where those who have trusted Jesus will live in the future (John 14:2). Gary Habermas writes that "the life of heaven is eternal life." And it isn't merely a continuation of our life now. There will be no sorrow, crying, or pain in heaven, and the inhabitants of heaven will never again experience death (Revelation 21:4).

> *Your place in heaven will seem to be made for you and you alone, because you were made for it.*
>
> —C. S. Lewis

"Heaven will be a place of great activity," asserts Habermas. True believers will see Jesus face-to-face in heaven and be able to interact with Him (1 John 3:2). In fact, believers will be *glorified*—that is, raised with Jesus, seated and exalted with Him in heaven (Ephesians 2:6). While we're there, we will serve God (Revelation 5:10) and give praise to Jesus, the Lamb who is worthy (Revelation 5:12).

"What Happens When Christians Die?"

The Bible is pretty clear that when Christians die, they immediately go into the presence of the Lord. When the thief on the cross said, "Jesus, remember me when you come into your Kingdom," Jesus told him he would be in "paradise" that very day (Luke 23:43). And Paul wrote that he longed "to go and be with Christ" (Philippians 1:23). However, departed Christians will not receive a glorified body until the future resurrection at the rapture. Theologians call this time between a believer's death and resurrection the "intermediate state." According to J. P. Moreland, even though the body has died, the believer's eternal soul exists in a conscious state and enjoys fellowship with God in real time while waiting for a new, resurrected body.

According to Habermas and many other writers, we will be reunited with our believing loved ones who died before us (Matthew 8:11). In heaven, we will be able to grow in knowledge and truth, "thereby increasing our awareness of God and his works."

Is that enough to get your juices flowing? Hey, we're just getting started! Let's look at some of these aspects of heaven in more detail.

Heaven Is a Place

In certain circles—including some religious ones—it is fashionable (or should we say, politically correct) to deny that a real heaven exists in a real place. Instead, the argument goes, heaven is a state of mind—if it exists at all. Other people criticize thoughts about heaven as being "wishful thinking." To believe in heaven, they say, is to believe in fairy tales.

Don't be fooled. Heaven is not an alternative to reality. Heaven *is* reality. C. S. Lewis put it this way:

> *If Heaven is not real, every honest person will disbelieve in it simply for that reason, however desirable it is, and if it is real, every honest man, woman, child, scientist, theologian, saint, and sinner will want to believe in it simply because it is real, not just because it is desirable.*

If heaven is *real*, then it is a *real place*. Jesus confirmed this when He said:

> *There are many rooms in my Father's home, and I am going to prepare a place for you. If this were not so, I would tell you plainly. When everything is ready, I will come and get you, so that you will always be with me where I am. And you know where I am going and how to get there* (John 14:2-4).

Just like Disney World

You've seen the television ads. Moments after some team wins the Super Bowl, an off-camera announcer says, "Tank Ridgerock, you're the champion of the world. Now what are you going to do?" To which Tank replies, "I'm going to Disney World!" as if that would be *the* ultimate destination.

Well, we admit that going to Disney World is pretty cool, so we would like to draw a comparison between the Magic Kingdom and God's kingdom.

What's fun about Disney World is that when you get there, you've got lots to do. You aren't stuck with just one ride or just one area to explore, unlike your crummy little county fair back home. You've got a choice of different lands or themes. Well, we would like to propose that heaven is a place with different lands. So let's take a tour of what heaven will include.

A New Heaven and a New Earth

Several times the Bible asserts that after the end of the world as we know it there will be "a new heaven and a new earth." According to both Berkhof and Thiessen, the old earth and heaven won't be completely destroyed, but rather regenerated. The process will begin during the millennium (see chapter 7), and will be completed after the millennium and the great white throne judgment.

**Chapter
7**

Then I saw a new heaven and a new earth, for the old heaven and the old earth had disappeared (Revelation 21:1).

Thiessen believes it will go something like this: At the conclusion of the millennium, when Christ has conquered all His enemies—including Satan and death—He will turn the kingdom over to God the Father.

After that the end will come, when he will turn the Kingdom over to God the Father, having put down all enemies of every kind. For Christ must reign until he humbles all his enemies beneath his feet. And the last enemy to be destroyed is death. . . . Then, when he has conquered all things, the Son will present himself to God, so that God, who gave his Son authority over all things, will be utterly supreme over everything everywhere (1 Corinthians 15:24-28).

Because of what Christ has done on the cross to make all this possible, God will in turn elevate His Son to the highest place in heaven and earth. In fact, He's already done it.

Because of this, God raised him up to the heights of heaven and gave him a name that is above every other name, so that at the name of Jesus every knee will bow, in heaven and on earth and under the earth, and every tongue will confess that Jesus Christ is Lord, to the glory of God the Father (Philippians 2:9-11).

That's why all the inhabitants and hosts of heaven will worship Jesus, the Lamb who is worthy (Revelation 5:11-14).

Can you get the picture that heaven as a *place* will include both a new heaven—which we have never seen—and also a new earth—a shadow of which we have seen? We do. If you've ever been at the top of Niagara Falls or gazed up at Half Dome in Yosemite, you have probably experienced a tiny glimpse of heaven.

A New City

A lot of people love the country, but not everyone. Some prefer cities. They love the excitement, the lights, the streets, and the glamour. Yet even the biggest proponents of city life are always a little leery of the potential dangers (such as being mugged or run over by a taxi).

Did you know that heaven will include a city? It's called the New Jerusalem, and it's described in detail in Revelation 21:

> And I saw the holy city, the new Jerusalem, coming down from God out of heaven like a beautiful bride prepared for her husband. I heard a loud shout from the throne, saying, "Look, the home

---

Angels in Heaven

The popular image which suggests that people turn into angels upon arrival in heaven, where they strum harps while floating on clouds, is nowhere to be found in the Bible. Instead, angels are created, nonhuman beings who exist to serve and praise God. They are stationed in heaven now (after all, they are the *heavenly* host), and they will be in the new heaven with believers. Together we will sing praises to the Lamb and to God (Revelation 5:11-14).

*of God is now among his people! He will live with
them, and they will be his people. God himself will be
with them"* (Revelation 21:2,3).

Isn't that awesome? You really need to read all of
Revelation 21, because this is where we get the idea
that the streets of heaven will be made of gold and
the gates of heaven will be made of pearls. There's no
doubt that the New Jerusalem is a literal city, probably the city that Abraham hoped for.

*Abraham . . . was confidently looking forward to a
city with eternal foundations, a city designed and
built by God* (Hebrews 11:10).

It's also the city that *we* long for.

*For this world is not our home; we are looking for-
ward to our city in heaven, which is yet to come*
(Hebrews 13:14).

This city is heaven, but it's not all of heaven. Think of
the New Jerusalem as the capital city of heaven. Like
the Cinderella castle at Disney World, this celestial
city will be visible from all parts of the new heaven
and the new earth. And just like Disney World, you'll
be able to move from one part of heaven to another
(only a lot faster and there won't be any lines!).

Heaven Is a State

When we say that heaven is a state, we don't mean
that heaven is a place like Missouri. By *state* we mean

GLAD YOU ASKED *"Is There a First, Second, and Third Heaven?"*

The Bible talks about the "third heaven" only once (2 Corinthians 12:2), but it never mentions a first or second heaven, so theologians can only speculate. Merrill Unger believes the *first* heaven is within the earth's atmosphere, while the *second* heaven describes space. The *third* heaven is where God and God alone lives. This would be the heaven that Jesus is preparing for all believers.

that heaven will offer opportunities far beyond anything we can imagine. Habermas writes that speaking of heaven as a state "encompasses all of the rich blessings not true of earth, including intimate knowledge of God and fellowship with him." This is where your thoughts about heaven can really begin to expand.

One of the incredible things about heaven is that we will continue to grow in knowledge and truth. Peter Kreeft writes that when we get to heaven, we will begin "the endless and endlessly fascinating task of exploring, learning, and loving the facets of infinity, the inexhaustible nature of God." We will not be omniscient—that is, know everything—but we will continue to learn throughout eternity: things about heaven, about each other, and about God.

Heaven will also provide several conditions we can only dream about now. Take note of the fact that though we experience each of these in some measure now, we always fall short of being able to enjoy them completely. Habermas presents five images from the Bible that help us to see what it might be like when we experience heaven:

1. We will have complete *peace* (Psalm 23:1-3). We long for peace in our world, we long for peace in our relationships, and we long for peace of mind. Even though it is impossible to experience complete peace in a world characterized by conflict, we know enough of what peace feels like to long for it. In heaven we will experience total, wonderful, blissful peace because God will care for our every need. For a beautiful picture of what this will feel like, read Psalm 23.

2. We will have complete *rest* (Psalm 91:1). Everybody's tired. Sometimes the greatest longing we have is for a good night's sleep. Even more than rest from physical weariness, we desire rest from our daily stress and pressures. Think of it! In heaven we will have complete rest, because God will have removed all our burdens. Our bodies will be continuously fresh, our minds always sharp, and our hearts forever light.

3. We will have complete *security* and *protection* (Psalm 91:2). We worry so much about security. Consequently, we take great measures to protect our person and our possessions. But even then, there's no guarantee that we will be completely safe. How would you feel if you were totally protected from harm of any kind, whether inflicted by people, animals, diseases, or disasters? That's what we'll have in heaven.

4. We will have complete *beauty* (Psalm 19:1). One of the unique qualities about being human is that you can appreciate beautiful things. You find joy in the beauty of nature. You recognize the beauty of great design and quality construction. But this is nothing compared to heaven. Heaven will provide a feast for the senses as we find ourselves surrounded by the natural beauty of the "paradise of God" (Revelation 2:7). As if that weren't enough, the wonders of the city "designed and built by God" will be yours to explore and enjoy for as long as you like.

5. We will have complete *fellowship* (Matthew 26:29). There's nothing sweeter than enjoying a delicious meal with family and friends (especially if *you* don't have to cook). More than once, Jesus used the image of sitting down together for a meal to describe heaven. He told His disciples that He was looking forward to having fellowship with them "in my Father's Kingdom." And Jesus has promised you that He will share a meal with you as a friend if you will just open the door of your heart and invite Him in (Revelation 3:20).

Can you imagine? The King of kings wants to sit down with you for a meal in heaven. The thought should take your breath away! Not only that, but when you are in heaven you will have the luxury of spending time with the people you love and care about, not to mention the incredible people in history you can only wonder about. It's true! Jesus said that we would be able to "sit down with Abraham, Isaac, and Jacob at the feast in the Kingdom of Heaven" (Matthew 8:11).

We could go on forever (no pun intended) because there's so much more to talk about. And you probably have a bunch of questions. So in the interest of time and space, here are some questions we think you might have about heaven.

Bruce and Stan's Ten Questions About Heaven

1. Will we have bodies in heaven?

Peter Kreeft, who has written two wonderful books about heaven, says that Christianity is the only belief system in which we "become more than we were before death." In every other belief system you are either gone forever (materialism), you become a spirit or ghost (pantheism), your consciousness becomes one with the cosmos (Buddhism), or you are reincarnated (Shirley MacLaine).

In Christianity, if you have received God's provision for salvation, you are guaranteed a resurrected, glorified body. Paul draws a remarkable contrast between our present bodies, which die and decay, and our resurrected bodies, which will be full of glory and power and will never die. "For our perishable earthly bodies must be transformed into heavenly bodies that will never die" (1 Corinthians 15:53). All of this is made possible by the resurrection of Jesus, who became "the first of a great harvest of those who will be raised to life again" (1 Corinthians 15:20).

Will our resurrected bodies bear the same imperfections and scars of our earthly bodies? That's hard to say. After His resurrection, Jesus asked doubting Thomas to place his hands into His scars. On the other hand, Kreeft writes that God is the author of healing. "Heaven will be the answer to every prayer, every desire for healing, physical, emotional, mental, and spiritual. All healings on earth are previews of coming attractions."

2. Will we recognize each other in heaven?

Again, the resurrected body of Christ provides us with some clues about our own resurrected bodies. Although His body was glorified, His disciples *did* recognize Him. Therefore, it seems logical to assume that we will also recognize each other in heaven. Jesus said as much to His disciples (Matthew 8:11). Besides, our fellowship with each other will be much more meaningful if we know each other.

A related question is, "What age will we be in heaven?" Will our resurrected bodies be the same age as when we die (or are raptured), or will we all be the same age? The Bible gives us no answer, so we can only speculate. We do know that since our heavenly bodies will not decay or die, they will not age. Perhaps we won't even see age. Kreeft points out Thomas Aquinas's belief that the perfect age was 33, which was the age of Christ when He died. "Therefore, he thought everyone would have a body like a thirty-three-year-old body in Heaven." Interesting thought.

3. Will there be time in heaven?

Now here's a topic that can get you thinking in circles! We must distinguish clearly between *chronos* time (earthly time measured by a clock) and *kairos* time (related to purpose and fulfillment, as in, "She had the time of her life"). Certainly there will be no *chronos* time in heaven, but it isn't correct to say there won't be *any* time in heaven.

Sometimes people confuse *eternity* with *timelessness*. We will live in eternity, or an eternal state, but only God is eternal. Only God has no beginning and no end (Revelation 1:17,18). Only God lives in the eternal *present*. When we're in heaven, we will experience time as a sequence of events.

Habermas calls this "a flow of heavenly time, including both past and future. Moments will be realized and will recede into the past, while others await us in our future." He prefers the term "endless time" to "timelessness."

4. Will we have emotions in heaven?

This is a pretty good question, because it covers two distinct issues. First, if we have emotions, will we be able to control them? Kreeft is confident we will have them, and that controlling them won't be an issue. "We will retain our feeling in heaven just as we will retain our thinking," he writes. "All our humanity is perfected, not diminished, in heaven."

But having emotions raises another tough question: Will we feel bad for loved ones who are in hell? This is a pretty tough one to answer, but again Kreeft offers a reasonable suggestion: "If our spirits are similar enough to God, we too can love without sorrow or vulnerability because we love only with the active feeling of caring, not with the passive feeling of being hurt." Habermas says that "we can be assured that God will be true to his Word—heaven will still be painless, in spite of the reality of hell and who resides there."

5. Will there be sex in heaven?

Oh boy, you had to ask, didn't you? Right away we think of the classic situation of the young Christian man who is looking forward to the Lord's return, but only wants it to happen *after* he gets married and has a chance to, well, you know, *consummate* his marriage. Actually, when you think about it, why wouldn't there be sex in heaven? After all, when it's expressed in the confines of marriage, sex is a wonderful thing created by God. And if our humanity is perfected in heaven, then why not perfect sex?

There's only one problem. Jesus was very specific on this issue when He said, "For when the dead rise, they won't be married. They will be like the angels in heaven" (Mark 12:25). Since God allows sex only in marriage, and there won't be any marriage in heaven, it doesn't look like there will be any sex either. But is this absence really that significant? Will not the love in heaven be so perfect that it will exceed even the imperfect love we knew in marriage?

*T*ime magazine asked 809 adults who believe in heaven to name four things that will be there. Ninety-three percent said angels, 79 percent said St. Peter, 43 percent said harps, and 36 percent said halos.

6. Will there be sin in heaven?

The easy answer is, "Of course not. We'll be perfect in heaven, incapable of sinning." But is that necessarily the case? The Bible is clear that the "unbelievers" and the "corrupt" will be in the "lake that burns with fire and sulfur" (Revelation 21:8), implying that the believers and those who are not corrupt will be in heaven. (The reason we will not be corrupt, of course, is that we believed and accepted Jesus, who paid the penalty for our sin). Therefore, there will be no sin in heaven.

But will we still be tempted to sin, in much the same way that Adam and Eve were tempted, even though they began their lives in a perfect condition? Will we have a free will in heaven, just like Adam and Eve? These are tough questions, but there are some reasonable answers. Habermas notes that we will still have free will, but since we will no longer have sin natures, we will *be able not to sin*, which is different than *not being able to sin*. "In this case," writes Habermas, "we would still be free to sin, but we would always choose not to because the glories and virtues of heaven would be so marvelous that no one in heaven would ever choose to act against those benefits."

Besides, the great tempter, Satan, will be spending eternity in the hothouse, so he won't be around to sneak up on us like the snake that he is.

7. Will everyone be equal in heaven?

This gets to the issue of blessings and rewards for deeds done on earth for Christ, which we covered in chapter 9. When the Bible talks about receiving a reward (1 Corinthians 3:14; Ephesians 6:8), it doesn't specify how that will play out in heaven. Habermas believes that "crowns have something to do with further spiritual development, learning, and service to the Lord." But if there are degrees of service in heaven, you can be sure that we won't be jealous or envious of one another, because such feelings are from the old sin nature.

8. Do people in heaven see us now?

How often do we say something like, "I'm sure Grandma is looking down on us right now." Even people who don't believe in a personal God will say stuff like that. Is it true? We've already said that after believers die, their souls and their consciousness—but not their bodies—go into the presence of the Lord. So can departed believers actually see us and know what we're doing? The Bible does say that "since we are surrounded by such a huge crowd of witnesses to the life of faith . . . let us run with endurance the race that God has set before us" (Hebrews 12:1). You get the picture that we are running a race called the Christian life, and the "witnesses" are departed saints cheering us from the sidelines. We know that the angels are watching us in real time (1 Corinthians 11:10), so why not the saints? Kreeft makes an interesting analogy to the body of Christ: "Christianity does not worship an absent Christ. And just as He can be on earth even when He has gone to Heaven, so can we—in Him. The cells in the one Body are all living cells, but only a very few of them are living on earth."

9. Will there be animals in heaven?

This is probably a very big question for many people. Often, to comfort children, we tell them that Fido, who has just been hit by a car, has gone to doggie heaven. Is there any merit to that child-like belief? Habermas doesn't think so, since the Bible doesn't say anything about it. Plus, we should remember that animals weren't created in the image of God, which means they don't have an eternal soul.

But Peter Kreeft answers this question by asking, "Why not?" He says that other nonhuman things will be in heaven (such as green fields and flowers), so why not animals? "Animals belong in the 'new earth' as much as trees," he writes. He also makes the point that human beings were meant, from the beginning, to have stewardship over the animals (Genesis 1:28). Since we have pretty much violated that divine directive on earth now, "it seems likely that the right relationship with animals will be part of Heaven."

10. Will we ever get bored in heaven?

There are two main reasons why this question gets asked. First, we have gotten awfully attached to this big blue marble called earth. Especially for those of us who live in the western world, life has been pretty good over the last few decades. We don't long for another world because we kind of like the one we have. Secondly, the thought that we will someday be in a place where we won't be able to do all the things we enjoy—and then have an endless amount of time *not* to do them—seems, well, boring.

We hope that if you ever had those thoughts, you are at least beginning to change your mind now that you've read this chapter. Because if you really believe that heaven exists, and that even *half* the stuff we have talked about in the chapter is really going to happen, then you have to believe that heaven will be the most exciting, invigorating, enriching, and entertaining place we humans could ever experience.

Habermas is excited by the idea that in heaven, with an endless amount of time at our disposal, we will be able to explore the Person of God, who is omnipotent, omniscient, and infinite. We will also be living "in God's newly created universe, which will be at our fingertips to explore and learn about." And we will have all the time we need to learn more and more about each other.

It's true that our present world is a pretty exciting place, but it pales in comparison to the world to come.

"What's That Again?"

1. The reason we hope for heaven is that we long for something better than this world.

2. Heaven is a real place created by God for all believers who have ever lived. It will be a place of great activity: We will worship Jesus, interact with others, and grow in knowledge.

3. Heaven will include a new heaven, a new earth, and the New Jerusalem.

4. In heaven we will experience complete peace, rest, security, beauty, and fellowship.

5. We will have bodies, recognize each other, and experience emotions as we spend eternity in heaven.

6. There will be no sin, sex, sorrow, or death in heaven (although there may be animals!).

7. We will never be bored in heaven.

Dig Deeper

Everything You Ever Wanted to Know About Heaven by Peter Kreeft. In this fun and creative book, Professor Kreeft will do more to open your imagination to heaven than any other writer, although you may not agree with every conclusion he reaches.

Heaven: Your Real Home by Joni Eareckson Tada. This recent book, by a woman bound to a wheelchair due to paralysis, offers unique insights into heaven. Joni paints a joyful and very personal portrait of her favorite place.

Beyond Death by Gary Habermas and J. P. Moreland. This is our favorite book on heaven and the afterlife—well-documented, scholarly, yet approachable. The two authors also talk about near-death experiences.

A History of Heaven by Jeffrey Burton Russell. Dr. Russell is known for his books about Satan and hell, which we've never read. But we can recommend this one on heaven. He traces the many different images of heaven that have appeared in literature and art through the centuries.

Someday Heaven by Larry Libby. This is a beautifully illustrated and well-written book for children. The author answers questions a child—and most adults, for that matter—would ask about heaven.

The Great Divorce by C. S. Lewis. The Oxford scholar often wrote about heaven, but he never devoted an entire book to the subject. This little books comes the closest. It is an allegorical account of a bus trip from hell to "the brightest borders of Heaven."

Moving On . . .

We hope that these chapters have given you a clearer picture of what to expect at the end of the world, culminating in the endless joy of heaven.

How do you feel about the end now? Take stock of your emotions. Are you more excited as the end of the world—or the end of your life, whichever comes first—gets closer each and every day? Or are you frightened? Maybe your emotions are mixed. That's okay. It's going to take some time to process your feelings as you think about everything we've said.

Besides yourself, you may be thinking about the people who are important to you. You may know where you're going to spend eternity, but do they? How can you convey your feelings and beliefs to someone you love who doesn't buy into your view of the end of the world?

In Part IV, we're going to address some of these issues. And we're going to help you apply what you know about the end of the world to your life now. So hang on.

PART IV:

What in the World Should We Do Now?

I wonder whether people who ask God to interfere openly and directly in our world quite realize what it will be like when He does. When that happens, it is the end of the world. When the author walks onto the stage, the play is over. God is going to invade, all right: but what is the good of saying you are on His side then, when you see the whole natural universe melting away like a dream and something else—something it never entered your head to conceive—comes crashing in; something so beautiful to some of us and so terrible to others that none of us will have any choice left? For this time it will be God without disguise; something so overwhelming that it will strike either irresistible love or irresistible horror into every creature. It will be too late then to choose your side. There is no use saying you choose to lie down when it has become impossible to stand up. That will not be the time for choosing: it will be the time when we discover which side we really have chosen, whether we realized it before or not. Now, today, this moment, is our chance to choose the right side. God is holding back to give us that chance. It will not last forever. We must take it or leave it.

—C. S. Lewis

We feel a special bond with you—the same sort we feel with our families after a summer vacation. You know the kind of vacations we mean, when fantastic and lousy things happen all in the same week, but you feel closer to each other because of all the experiences you shared. Well, that's how we feel about you. After all, look at what we have gone through together:

The rapture . . . the tribulation . . . the second coming . . . the final judgments. Hey, we've even been to heaven and hell together. That's even more adventure and anguish than you get on a cross-country road trip to Grandma Farley's in Indiana.

But let's not leave each other just yet. Even though our trip has come to an end, let's see if we are better or worse for having gone through the last few chapters. We don't have a photo album to help us relive our memories, but we can at least ask the question, "So what?"

You'll be deciding for yourself whether this information about the future is significant to *you*. But we thought that you might be interested in a few of *our* suggestions for how you can analyze all this data. After all, we've got quite a history in common with you . . . actually, we've got quite a future in common with you, too.

Bruce & Stan

Chapter 11

Act Now!
Limited Time Offer

. . . .

What's Ahead

➤ Now it's getting personal
➤ Knock, knock. Who's there?
➤ Knowing *your* future (absolutely, positively)
➤ What in the world are you waiting for?

. . . .

*I*f you have plowed through the preceding ten chapters, you know that the study of end-times prophecy (if done correctly) is tough work. We're sorry if that caught you by surprise. Maybe we told you too much. Maybe we didn't tell you enough. Maybe you just wanted to know an exact date so you could make an entry in your Daytimer for "the world ends today" (and we *especially* didn't tell you that).

In fact, you may have more questions now than when you started. And given the obscure nature of prophecy, you probably do. Even if you don't think you know a lot about this subject, you know enough to realize that *you* have a big decision to make—a decision that will determine *your* future destiny.

Now It's Getting Personal

We've mostly been talking on a global scale over the past several chapters: what happens in the universe, what happens to the planet, what happens to the human race, etc. On this level, what we have been saying could seem kind of impersonal. But don't get the wrong impression. You cannot be a disinterested bystander or merely an observer on the sidelines. Like it or not, you are an active participant, and God's plan for the world revolves around *you*.

Every verse in the Bible which talks about humanity applies to *you* personally. So here is what you can find out about yourself by reading the Bible:

✓ *You* are a sinner, and *you* can never satisfy God's standard of holiness.

> *For all have sinned; all fall short of God's glorious standard* (Romans 3:23).

✓ The consequences of *your* sin mean that *you* deserve the penalty of eternal death.

> *For the wages of sin is death* (Romans 6:23).

✓ Christ did something for *you* that *you* could never do for *your-self*: He paid the penalty for *your* sins by dying on the cross.

> *But God showed his great love for us by sending Christ to die for us while we were still sinners* (Romans 5:8).

> *I*t is so easy to receive Christ that millions stumble over its sheer simplicity.
>
> —Billy Graham

✓ *You* can be saved from the penalty of sin by believing in Jesus.

For if you confess with your mouth that Jesus is Lord and believe in your heart that God raised him from the dead, you will be saved (Romans 10:9).

✓ That's all that is required of you. There's nothing else. Salvation is God's free gift.

God saved you by his special favor when you believed. And you can't take credit for this; it is a gift from God (Ephesians 2:8).

✓ There is no other way for *you* to have eternal life with God. It can only come through Jesus.

Jesus told him, "I am the way, the truth, and the life. No one can come to the Father except through me" (John 14:6).

Knock, Knock. Who's There?

We hope you have the correct impression about God. He is not some stuffy, old cosmic curmudgeon who will make you come crawling and begging to be accepted by Him. It is just the opposite. He is politely (but anxiously) waiting for you to invite Him into your life. In the Book of Revelation, the apostle John describes a very poignant vision of Christ standing at the door of our life:

The Whole Bible in One Verse

If we had to pick one verse to summarize the whole Bible, it would be John 3:16. Look at how it covers all the key elements about sin, salvation, and eternal life in the future. And observe at how it relates directly to *you*:

> *For God so loved the world* . . . [That certainly includes you.]
>
> *that he gave his only Son...*[Christ was the only perfect Person, the only One who could die for the sins of others.]
>
> *so that everyone who believes in him...*[That includes you again.]
>
> *will not perish but have eternal life.* [This is how your future can change from hell to heaven.]

Look! Here I stand at the door and knock. If you hear me calling and open the door, I will come in, and we will share a meal as friends (Revelation 3:20).

Christ is waiting for you to respond to His offer of salvation. In fact, the apostle Peter said that God is holding back the events of the end of the world in order to give you an opportunity to respond:

The Lord isn't really being slow about his promise to return, as some people think. No, he is being patient for your sake. He does not want anyone to perish, so he is giving more time for everyone to repent (2 Peter 3:9).

Knowing Your Future (Absolutely, Positively)

Your sin condemns you to hell. There is no doubt about that. But if you believe in Christ as your Savior, then your sins are forgiven by God and you are bound for heaven at the end of your life. That result is equally certain. But what if you sin again after you have believed in Christ? Have you suddenly derailed off the track to heaven? Will your "gift of salvation" be snatched from your grasp and given to someone more deserving?

First of all, no one *deserves* God's gift of salvation. So you don't have to worry about someone else being better than you. Secondly, you don't have to worry whether you are going to sin again—you will (although you should see improvement as you learn to resist your natural instincts and respond to circumstances from a Christian perspective). Thirdly, God is not going to revoke your salvation once He has given it to you.

Think about this: If a sin can cancel a believer's salvation, then Christ's sacrifice on the cross wasn't sufficient to cover that sin. But Christ's death on the

Being a Christian Means . . .

What does it mean to be a Christian? We like this definition: a fully devoted follower of Christ. Here are a few other terms which might be helpful to you:

Belief. Christianity means believing in Christ. But believing is more than merely giving intellectual assent to God's existence. (Even Satan and the demons believe that Jesus is God's Son.) It means being convinced that His death on the cross was sufficient to pay the penalty for your sins.

Faith. A Christian is one who has faith that God knows what is best, so a Christian turns ownership and control of his or her life over to God. We don't become robots, but our perspective changes from being self-centered to being God-centered.

Repentance. Being sorry for your sins isn't enough. A Christian has a sincere desire to refrain from sin in the future. True repentance means that you turn away from a life-style which is not pleasing to God.

Being a Christian Doesn't Mean . . .

A lot of people base their opinion of Christianity on a few poor examples. But you should evaluate something by a good example of it, not a bad one. (So don't evaluate opera by listening to Stan sing, or basketball by watching Bruce dribble and jump.) Don't be turned off to Christianity because you think it means you have to be . . .

Fanatical. Thumping people on their heads with a Bible is not required. You should expect to be enthusiastic, but all God asks is that you be genuine.

Brain-dead. When you become a Christian, you don't have to kiss your brains good-bye. Christianity can easily withstand an intellectual investigation. God wants you to love Him with your heart *and* your mind.

Superreligious. You don't have to live in a monastery. You can have fun and enjoy life. You don't even have to use "thees and thous."

Republican. We are sure Jesus wants Christians in both political parties.

It Isn't Just About the Future

Eternal life with God in heaven is not the only benefit of believing in Christ. There is also a "here and now" benefit. Through the Holy Spirit which lives inside every believer, your life will be transformed to manifest the very characteristics of God Himself:

> *But when the Holy Spirit controls our lives, he will produce this kind of fruit in us: love, joy, peace, patience, kindness, goodness, faithfulness, gentleness, and self-control* (Galatians 5:22,23).

cross *was* great enough to cover all the sins of all people for all times. Once you are saved, your membership in God's family cannot be broken. Your eternal life is sealed forever.

And I am convinced that nothing can ever separate us from his love. Death can't, and life can't. The angels can't, and the demons can't. Our fears for today, our worries about tomorrow, and even the powers of hell can't keep God's love away. Whether we are high above the sky or in the deepest ocean, nothing in all creation will ever be able to separate us from the love of God that is revealed in Christ Jesus our Lord (Romans 8:38,39).

What in the World Are You Waiting For?

How are you going to respond to Christ's invitation of eternal life? There is no way for us to know. (Actually, there is. Our web site, e-mail and postal addresses are listed in the introduction. We would love to hear from you.) But even if we never meet, we guess that you must fall into one of six categories.

The Rejecter

Maybe you're saying, "Nope! This Christianity stuff is not for me." Well, that's not the decision which we would hope you would make, but we respect your right to choose for yourself. And so does God. After all, He was the One who gave you a free will in the first place.

If you are in this category, we hope that you analyze the basis for your decision. Don't rely on what other people say (even us). Check things out for yourself. If you need more information, get it. But whatever you do, don't say that there is not enough proof about God. You already have all the proof you need.

> For the truth about God is known to them instinctively. God has put this knowledge in their hearts. From the time the world was created, people have seen the earth and sky and all that God made. They can clearly see his invisible qualities—his eternal power and divine nature. So they have no excuse whatsoever for not knowing God (Romans 1:19-20).

This decision is too important to evaluate on the basis of a hunch.

The Debater

Maybe you have some objections. Perhaps you have argued a few points with a Christian who crumbled under your cross-examination. Don't make the mistake of thinking that Christianity is flawed simply because there are parts of it that seem foolish to you. Remember that your eternal salvation does not depend upon God explaining everything to your satisfaction. If you could figure out everything about Him, then *you* would be God.

> *I know very well how foolish the message of the cross sounds to those who are on the road to destruction. . . . As the Scriptures say, "I will destroy human wisdom and discard their most brilliant ideas." So where does this leave the philosophers, the scholars, and the world's brilliant debaters? God has made them all look foolish and has shown their wisdom to be useless nonsense* (1 Corinthians 1:18-20).

The Deliberator

You are in this category if you have "analysis paralysis." You just can't make up your mind.

✓ You want to turn your life over to Christ, but you don't want to lose your freedom.

✓ It all seems to make sense to you, but you don't know where it will lead.

*W*e cannot pander to a man's intellectual arrogance, but we must cater to his intellectual integrity.

—John Stott

✓ You are afraid of going to hell after death, but you are afraid that Christianity might kill your life-style now.

Just be honest with yourself. Decide what is really holding you back, and ask yourself if it is worth it.

> *A doubtful mind is as unsettled as a wave of the sea that is driven and tossed by the wind. People like that should not expect to receive anything from the Lord. They can't make up their minds. They waver back and forth in everything they do* (James 1:6-8).

The Procrastinator

You're the one who says, "I've got plenty of time to decide. I'll make the decision later." This category may be the most dangerous of all, because you don't realize that making no decision has the same effect as rejecting Christ.

You don't control the clock or the calendar for making your decisions. Just as "no one knows the hour" of Christ's return, you don't know the time of your death. It may happen when you least expect it, and you will spend an eternity in hell regretting that you postponed your decision to accept Christ. You will be like the rich fool in Jesus' parable who thought he had his life all planned out:

> *But God said to him, "You fool! You will die this very night"* (Luke 12:20).

The events of the end times are cloaked with a sense of suddenness and surprise. Christ's return is described as occurring with the stealth of a "thief in the night." Your ability to make a decision at a later time may be unexpectedly cut short by death. After that, you'll have an eternity of time to ponder the decision which you never made.

The Imitator

Don't get the idea that you can fake your way into heaven. You can pretend to be religious, but pretending doesn't cut it. Salvation doesn't depend on how often you went to church, how much you gave to charity, and whether or not you wore clean underwear on Sundays. All of that stuff is external. It's on the outside. God cares about what is in your heart.

> The LORD doesn't make decisions the way you do! People judge by outward appearance, but the LORD looks at a person's thoughts and intentions (1 Samuel 16:7).

Other people may think that you are a Christian, but God will know the truth. You can't hide it from Him. All of your religious activity will be meaningless on judgment day if you are not a true believer.

> Not all people who sound religious are really godly. They may refer to me as "Lord," but they still won't enter the Kingdom of Heaven. The decisive issue is whether they obey my Father in heaven. On judgment day many will tell me, "Lord, Lord, we prophesied in your name and cast out demons in your name and performed many miracles in your name." But I will reply, "I never knew you. Go away; the things you did were unauthorized" (Matthew 7:21-23).

The Believer

This is the best of the possible positions. It is our sincere hope that you find the Bible to be reliable, and that you accept Christ as your Savior. At some point in your life you "asked Christ into your heart" by a simple prayer in which you expressed sorrow for your sins and turned control of your life over to God. If you are new to all of this, you are in for an experience which is out of this world (literally).

No eye has seen, no ear has heard, and no mind has imagined what God has prepared for those who love him (1 Corinthians 2:9).

"What's That Again?"

1. God's plan for the world involves *you*.

2. God offers salvation to you as a free gift. With it comes a new spiritual life on earth, and eternal life with God.

3. The decision is totally yours. You accept Christ by believing and trusting in Him. You reject Christ by doing nothing.

4. You don't have forever to make up your mind. But the results of your decision, or your failure to make one, will last forever.

Dig Deeper

Know Why You Believe by Paul Little. This is a classic book for examining legitimate questions about the Christian faith. Do science and Scripture conflict? Are miracles possible? Why does God allow suffering? These are questions which occur to seekers and believers alike, and Little provides solid answers.

Bruce & Stan's Guide to God by us. You might find chapter 9 ("Salvation: You Gotta Have Faith") to be particularly relevant on the subject of becoming a Christian. Chapter 12 ("The Christian Life: Where Do We Grow from Here?") discusses some important "next steps" for being a Christian.

A Ready Defense by Josh McDowell. If you are a skeptic and curious about the Christian faith, this book is for you! McDowell handles the most frequently asserted challenges to Christianity. This is also a good book for Christians who want to learn how to defend their beliefs.

Moving On . . .

For those of you who *are* Christians, you might be wondering what you should do next. You have studied the prophecies about the end times, and now you know that the rapture could happen at any moment. The events of the tribulation could begin very soon, and all hell will be breaking loose.

Should you stop paying your taxes because the rapture might happen before April 15? Should you move to a monastery where you will be insulated from the evils of ATMs, cable television, and caffeine additives?

May we suggest something far less drastic: Calmly turn the page and read chapter 12.

Chapter 12

Don't Wait Until You Are
Dead to Get a Life

Any theology that does not live with a sense of the immediate return of Christ is a theology that takes the edge off the urgency of faith. But any theology that does not cause us to live as though the world will be here for thousands of years is a theology that leads us into social irresponsibility.

—*Tony Campolo*

We would like to conclude our book with a special chapter just for believers. If you've responded to God's gracious offer of salvation and made the choice to invite Jesus into your heart—whether years ago or since you started reading this book—this chapter is especially for you.

We want to bring all of this end-of-the-world stuff back down to where it affects everyday living. We want to show you from Scripture how you can be heavenly minded here on earth. It's true that your future is secure, but there are some things God wants to do in you and through you right now.

Bruce & Stan

Chapter 12

Don't Wait Until You Are Dead to Get a Life

What's Ahead

➤ You have another choice to make
➤ Living your life from an earthly perspective
➤ Living your life from a heavenly perspective
➤ Bringing heaven to earth
➤ Becoming a kingdom person

*G*ospel music is filled with images that people use to describe what it will be like to go from this life into the next. Maybe you'll recognize some of these titles:

> "I'll Fly Away"
> "Cross Over Jordan"
> "The Unclouded Day"
> "Beyond the Sunset"
> "Glory Train"

When it comes to describing the Christian life, we especially like the train analogy because it illustrates that all believers are—

✓ Going from one place (eternal destruction) to another (eternal life)

✓ Traveling at ground level (we're still *in* the world).

✓ Making stops along the way (the journey isn't nonstop).

✓ Assured of our final destination (the glory train only travels on one track).

If only the Christian life were simply a matter of getting on the glory train, choosing a seat in the observation lounge, curling up with a good book, and making ourselves comfortable as we wait for that final stop where we will get off the world and arrive in heaven.

But the Christian life isn't like that. Even though the Conductor has punched your ticket to your final destination, and even though this old world is no longer your real home, you haven't yet reached the end of the line. You're still on the journey called life, and your future home with Jesus waits for you in the future. As the poem goes, you still have some miles to go before you sleep.

You Have Another Choice to Make

In the last chapter we emphasized that everyone has the choice of being a rejecter, a debater, a deliberater, a procrastinator, an imitator, or a believer. This choice, of course, occurs *before* you become a believer. Once you believe in Jesus as your Savior, you take on a new identity. You literally become a new person:

What this means is that those who become Christians become new persons. They are not the same anymore, for the old life is gone. A new life has begun! (2 Corinthians 5:17).

In addition to a new identity, you are immediately given a new citizenship:

We are citizens of heaven, where the Lord Jesus Christ lives (Philippians 3:20).

In reality, you have a *dual* citizenship. You're a citizen of heaven, but at the same time you're still a citizen of earth. More correctly, you are a *foreign* citizen on earth (1 Peter 2:11). In a way, you're like an *alien* with a green card (we're talking about earthly aliens of the working kind, although a case could be made for the other kind of alien, since you are a citizen of an extraterrestrial place).

You Have Two Choices

Once you have attained your dual citizenship, you must live your life in a kind of tension between your permanent future home and your temporary earthly one. Your choice to believe in Jesus resulted in your heavenly citizenship. But while you're still here on earth, you have another choice you need to make:

How am I going to live?

Here you have only two choices:

✓ **Choice #1–Living your life from an earthly perspective**

✓ **Choice #2–Living your life from a heavenly perspective**

Let's look at the consequences of each of these choices.

Living Your Life from an Earthly Perspective—Living with Fear

If there's one word that best characterizes life from an earthly perspective, it's *fear*. More specifically, it's the *fear of loss*. Here's what we mean: When you live life from an earthly perspective, you think the same way that the world thinks. And since the world is totally self-centered and has nothing eternal to offer, you are reduced to worrying about your *stuff* and your physical *self*, both of which are temporary and earthbound.

The Fear of Losing Your Stuff

First of all, you fear losing your *stuff*. You have possessions, which are neither good nor bad in themselves. It really doesn't make any difference if what you own would barely fill a shopping cart, or if you have so much stuff that you need a warehouse to hold it all. When you live life from an earthly perspective, you don't want to lose *any* of it. And because you are afraid that you might, you take whatever measures are necessary to protect and insure your stuff.

The Fear of Losing Your Self-esteem

You also have an ego, and you'll do just about anything to protect it. You care about your reputation, about what people think and say about you. You also care about success, wanting to avoid failure. Failure is one of your greatest fears, especially when you live your life from an earthly perspective.

The Fear of Losing Your Health

No one wants to get sick. It is one of our greatest worries. No one wants to experience pain. But even if you work hard to keep healthy, you still live with the fear that something might happen. When you live life from an earthly perspective, it is easy to become obsessed with being healthy.

The Fear of Losing Your Life

Read the headlines in any city and you'll see the same reports. Daily, people lose their lives through accidents, disease, and violence. No matter how great the precautions are that you take, you must always know that you could be next. This fear can be paralyzing when you look at life from an earthly perspective.

As a believer, it's not wrong to fear, but it is wrong to live in the grip of fear. In other words, if fear characterizes your life, it means you are living your life from an earthly perspective. It means you

> *A*s a Christian, this life is all the hell I shall ever experience. If I were a non-Christian, this life is all the heaven I shall ever experience.
>
> —Former U.S. Senator Harold Hughes

Fear Will Cause You to Sink

There's a great story in the New Testament (Matthew 14:22-33, to be exact) that illustrates the danger of fear. The disciples were trying to get from one side of the Sea of Galilee to the other when a big storm kicked up some heavy waves. Just when it seemed the boat was about to capsize, they saw Jesus walking toward them on the water. Of course, this freaked them out and the disciples screamed out in terror (they were afraid). Jesus comforted them, calling out, "It's all right, I am here! Don't be afraid."

Then Peter, the impulsive disciple, decided he couldn't wait for Jesus to get to the boat, so he stepped out and started to walk on the water toward Jesus. He was doing fine as long as he kept his eyes on Jesus, but when he looked around and saw the strength of the waves, he was filled with fear and began to sink. "Save me," Peter yelled out. Jesus grabbed him by the hand, pulled him to the top of the water once again, and said, "You don't have much faith. Why did you doubt me?"

The lesson for us is that fear comes from a lack of faith. Fear comes when we take our eyes off the Savior and start worrying about our circumstances.

have your eyes on the things of earth rather than the things of heaven. You are trusting yourself rather than trusting Jesus.

You see, that's the way the people without Jesus conduct their lives. They are earthbound, without any other options. They have no choice but to protect themselves and their stuff while they work to accumulate more. Here's what Jesus had to say about such a perspective:

> *How do you benefit if you gain the whole world but lose or forfeit your own soul in the process?* (Luke 9:25).

IF YOU'RE GOING TO FEAR SOMETHING, FEAR GOD

What do you think of when you hear the expression, "Fear God"? If you're living life from an earthly perspective, you will probably identify with the verse, "It is a terrible thing to fall into the hands of the living God" (Hebrews 10:31). But if you choose to live your life from a heavenly perspective, the meaning of "Fear God" takes on a much different—though no less important—meaning. We like what Chuck Swindoll said about it: "To fear God means to take Him seriously and do what He says." As a Christian, the first step in living your life from God's perspective is to do just that.

Living Your Life from a Heavenly Perspective—Living with Faith

The other choice for the Christian (keep in mind that only Christians have this choice) is to live your life from a heavenly perspective. This means seeing life from God's viewpoint rather than your own. It's living a life of *faith* rather than a life of *fear*.

We cannot emphasize enough just how important this is. "The God of the universe," writes Habermas, "invites you to view life and death from his eternal vantage point." This isn't a farfetched idea for people who would rather live with their heads in the clouds. It's what God calls us to in His Word:

> *Let heaven fill your thoughts. Do not think only about things down here on earth* (Colossians 3:2).

Do you really believe in heaven? Are you convinced that heaven is a real place? (Just in case you've forgotten our arguments, refer back to chapter 10.) If you really are sure about heaven, then you should have the ability to see things from a heavenly perspective. Don't worry about being "too heavenly minded to be any earthly good." You need to be *more* heavenly minded, not less. It's time to let *faith* characterize your life rather than *fear*.

Chapter 10

> *What is faith? It is the confident assurance that what we hope for is going to happen. It is the evidence of things we cannot yet see* (Hebrews 11:1).

Let Your Future Revolutionize Your Present

Thinking about heaven and viewing your life from God's eternal perspective will revolutionize the way you live. How? By helping you deal with your fear and with all those things you're afraid you're going to lose.

Your stuff. Jesus was very clear in His teachings about stuff. Actually, Jesus never used the word *stuff,* but He did talk about our possessions when He said:

> *So I tell you, don't worry about everyday life—whether you have enough food, drink, and clothes. Doesn't life consist of more than food and clothing?* (Matthew 6:25).

When you live your life from a heavenly perspective, you begin to see that your possessions ultimately belong to God in the first place. They are yours to manage, not to own. You shouldn't get too attached to them.

> *Don't store up treasures here on earth, where they can be eaten by moths and get rusty, and where thieves break in and steal. Store your treasures in heaven, where they will never become moth-eaten or rusty and where they will be safe from thieves. Wherever your treasure is, there your heart and thoughts will also be* (Matthew 6:19,20).

Seven Things That Will Last Forever

✓ Your eternal soul

✓ Relationships

✓ The Bible

✓ Treasures stored in heaven

✓ God's love

✓ The investment you make in other people

✓ Fruitcake

Your self-esteem. Once, some of Jesus' disciples were arguing about who was going to be the greatest in the "coming Kingdom." In worrying about this, they were looking at themselves from an earthly perspective. Knowing their hearts, Jesus said, "In this world the kings and great men order their people around" (Luke 22:25). Then He told them how to live with a heavenly perspective:

> But among you, those who are the greatest should take the lowest rank, and the leader should be like a servant (Luke 22:26).

Both your fear of losing your self-esteem and your fear of failure will melt away when you adopt the heavenly perspective of serving others.

"Aren't We Supposed to Take Care of Our Bodies?"

To not worry about your body is not the same thing as not caring. Your physical body is God's precious gift to you—the gift of life. Your physical body has a very important job. It has to carry around your eternal soul! That's why the Bible asks,

Don't you know that your body is a temple of the Holy Spirit, who lives in you and was given to you by God? You do not belong to yourself, for God bought you with a high price. So you must honor God with your body (1 Corinthians 6:19,20).

Your health. The heavenly perspective on health is very simple. You can certainly help maintain your health by taking care of your body. But from the view of eternity, you must remember that your body is in a state of decay. As you get older, you will become more susceptible to aches and pains and disease. This is the natural order of things. Sometimes even young bodies break down. But should this reality cause you to lose hope? No, it actually should give you the motivation to press on!

That is why we never give up. Though our bodies are dying, our spirits are being renewed every day. For

our present troubles are quite small and won't last very long. Yet they produce for us an immeasurably great glory that will last forever! (2 Corinthians 4:16,17).

Your life. Your own life may not be in any immediate danger, but don't forget that there are many Christians throughout the world who find themselves in that position on a regular basis. Earlier in this book we referred to the persecuted church and the many millions of Christians in other parts of the globe who literally risk their lives daily because of their faith.

We all are faced with the reality that we will someday die. You may be one who fears that you will die "before your time." But what is "your time"? From an earthly perspective there are certainly no guarantees. But from heaven's perspective, the guarantee is absolute. For the Christian, death is a doorway to glory.

When this happens—when our perishable earthly bodies have been transformed into heavenly bodies that will never die—then at last the Scriptures will come true: "Death is swallowed up in victory. O death, where is your victory? O death, where is your sting?" (1 Corinthians 15:54,55).

Bringing Heaven to Earth

As a Christian, you have another important responsibility while you're living here on this planet: *bringing heaven to earth.*

Jesus emphasized this when He told His disciples how to pray (in what is known as the Lord's Prayer). We're not going to give you the entire prayer here— just these words:

> *May your kingdom come soon. May your will be done here on earth, just as it is in heaven* (Matthew 6:10).

Jesus was making a connection between the kingdom of heaven that is coming and the spiritual kingdom which is real now in our hearts (see chapter 8). As believers, we are the link between the two. We are given the responsibility of bringing heaven to earth.

Dave Vasquez, a pastor friend of ours, once explained how this happens in a message called "Heaven on Earth" (it's amazing what you can learn when you go to church!). According to Vasquez, there are three ways God uses us to bring heaven to earth.

God with Us

God dwells in heaven, but one of His desires is to live with His human creations on earth. He walked with Adam and Eve in the garden (Genesis 3:8) and was with them on earth until sin broke their fellowship. God then established a people for Himself on earth (the Hebrews) and instructed them to build a tabernacle, which He filled with His presence (Exodus 40:34). When His people rebelled, God broke earthly contact once again.

Then, in God's most dramatic move, He came to earth in the form of a baby born to a virgin. He was called *Immanuel*, which literally means "God is with us" (Matthew 1:23). But once again, we rejected God's presence on earth, and He returned to heaven.

In His future kingdom, when He creates a new heaven and a new earth, God will once again live among His people (Revelation 21:3). In the meantime, God wants to live on earth *with* you. When you invited Jesus into your heart, God literally came through your heart's door to live within you (Revelation 3:20). You became a temple of the living God (2 Corinthians 6:16).

So the first way you bring heaven to earth is to invite Jesus into your heart.

God in Us

God wants to be *with* you, but He also wants to be *in* you. What's the difference? Maybe the best example is found in a romantic relationship between a woman and a man. It's one thing to be *with* another person. You tell people, "I really enjoy being with so-and-so." But at some point your feelings change. Something special happens between the two of you, and suddenly you start making comments like, "I feel like you're a part of me." Maybe old blue eyes, Frank Sinatra, said it best when he sang,

> *I've got you under my skin*
> *I've got you deep in the heart of me*
> *So deep in my heart that you're really a part of me.*

We don't mean to trivialize your relationship with God, but in order for you to really experience the dynamic power of God, He has to get under your skin. He has to get deep in your heart, where He can rule as Lord. That's where He wants to be: on the throne of your life. When this happens, your life will begin to impact the world around you. As people see God *in* you, they will begin to see God.

God Through Us

God is big on glory. His greatest desire is that we glorify Him. In the past, God has displayed His glory, particularly when Jesus came to earth (John 1:14). In the future, God's glory will be on full display when Jesus comes to reign on earth during the millennium (Matthew 19:28). But right now, He wants to display His glory *through* us by way of the good works produced in our lives.

Chapter 10

Remember how we described heaven (see chapter 10)? We said that heaven would be characterized by peace, rest, security, beauty, and fellowship. In heaven we will experience all these conditions perfectly, but that doesn't mean we can't experience them to some extent even while we are here on earth. As you allow God to work through you, He will bring these conditions into your life now and help you to bring them to others. That's what the apostle Paul meant when he wrote,

> *Sometimes I want to live, and sometimes I long to go and be with Christ. That would be far better for me, but*

it is better for you that I live. I am convinced of this, so I will continue with you so that you will grow and experience the joy of your faith (Philippians 1:23-25).

Becoming a Kingdom Person

You've got a *past* (God saved you), and you have a *future* (you will be with God at the end of the world). But right now, it's your job to bring God's presence to the *present*. You do this by becoming a kingdom person. As you grow in Christ and allow the Holy Spirit to work in you, you will exhibit more and more of the qualities God desires for you to show to the world.

Don't get discouraged if the process takes time. It will take a *lifetime*. But you will see progress. Here is God's guarantee:

> *As the Spirit of the Lord works within us, we become more and more like him and reflect his glory even more* (2 Corinthians 3:18).

May God bless you as you serve Him as a kingdom person.

"What's That Again?"

1. As a believer, you have a choice to make between living your life from an earthly or a heavenly perspective.

2. When you live your life from an earthly perspective, your life will be characterized by fear.

3. When you live your life from a heavenly perspective, your life will be characterized by faith.

4. You will bring heaven to earth as God works with you, in you, and through you.

5. Make it your goal to become a kingdom person.

Dig Deeper

There are so many wonderful books on how to live the Christian life (who knows, we may even write one ourselves someday). Here are a few favorites:

Basic Christianity by John R. W. Stott. If you only read one book on what it means to be a Christian, make this the one.

Authentic Christianity by Ray Stedman. An in-depth study of the idea that Jesus died *for* us so that He might live *in* us.

The Great House of God by Max Lucado. Because God wants to be your dwelling place, your home, Lucado uses the Lord's Prayer to show us what His house looks like.

Eternal Security by Charles Stanley. Sometimes believers question their salvation for various reasons. Dr. Stanley brings assurance that your salvation in Christ is complete and forever.

Moving On . . .

Congratulations! You've reached the end (of the book, not the world). We've given you a lot to think about, both about the world and your life. Our prayer is that you will use the information we've shared with you to live your life for Christ more faithfully and more urgently. If you haven't yet made the decision to follow Jesus, we hope that you will strongly consider your options for the future. But don't wait too long, because you never know . . .

The end of the world is coming soon
(1 Peter 4:7).

Think About It

As we have done in our other "Guide" books, we've come up with some thought-provoking questions for each chapter. If you're using this book in a group study, go through these together and give everyone a chance to answer each question. If you're doing a self-study, give yourself a chance to answer. In other words, don't skip this part. You may come up with answers you didn't know you had.

This isn't a final exam. There is no pass or fail, only the satisfaction of knowing that you know more about this subject now than you did before. We aren't going to send you a diploma for finishing the book or answering all of these questions, but you can write or e-mail us and ask us for an answer to one of *your* questions. The least we will do is write back (that's a promise).

Just in case you forgot where you saw our addresses (they are in the Introduction), here they are again: **e-mail** *guide@bruceandstan.com*, **web site** *www.bruceandstan.com*, **snail mail** P.O. Box 25565, Fresno, CA 93729-5565.

Chapter 1—The End Is Near . . . or Is It?

1. In what way is our world staying the same? Getting better? Getting worse? Would you agree that overall the world is getting worse? Why or why not?

2. Has there ever been a time in your life when you thought the world was about to end? Describe it.

3. How is it possible for you to be a positive Christian in the middle of a negative culture?

4. The year is 2050 and we're all still here. What will the world be like?

Chapter 2—Phonies, Flakes and Experts: Who Do You Trust?

1. Why are there so many phony options to the one true God?

2. Why do otherwise normal, intelligent, and successful people fall for psychics and other weird stuff?

3. Describe the power of the media now. How will the use of media increase in the future?

4. Does anyone or anything besides God stand up to Bruce & Stan's Truth Detector? Are you sure?

Chapter 3: The Bible: God's Handbook for the Past, Present, and Future

1. Write your own condensed version of the Bible. Forget about using stone tablets or parchment, just use a piece of paper and write a sentence or two which describes the major theme of the Bible. What is God's message to the human race?

2. God could have used many different forms of communication. Why do you suppose He used "the written word" as the primary means of presenting and preserving His message to mankind?

3. If you were a skeptic and refused to consider the Bible a reliable source for information concerning the future, what other resource is available? If you can think of any such resources, how do they compare to the Bible's track record?

Chapter 4: Reading the Bible for Fun and Prophet

1. Can you think of any other book which even comes close to making as many accurate predictions about the future as are contained in the Bible?

2. Why do you suppose that it was so important that the Old Testament prophets had to be 100% accurate and would be put to death if any one of their predictions turned out to be false?

3. The prophets did more than just make predictions. They also warned and encouraged people about their relationships with God. If you were a "present day" prophet, what would be your message to the people about their relationship with God?

Chapter 5: If It's God's Word, Why Is Everyone Arguing About It?

1. Why do people argue so vehemently over Bible prophecy? Can you think of another area of Scripture where people so sharply disagree?

2. How does the study of Bible prophecy give you a greater understanding of God's plan and purpose?

3. Which view—premillennialism, amillennialism, or postmillennialism—do you agree with? Does it matter to you?

Chapter 6: The Rapture: Now You See Me, Now You Don't

1. Put yourself in the place of the disciples when Jesus told them that He was going back to heaven, but would return later for them. What would you be thinking? What emotions would you be feeling?

2. Let your imagination run wild for a moment. Picture yourself as a television news reporter (who has no understanding of the biblical rapture). What events are you going to see and report in the moments following the actual occurrence of the rapture? What are you going to say in your commentary?

3. You might as well enter the debate (because everyone else has). Do you think that the rapture will occur before the tribulation, during the tribulation, or at the end of the tribulation? Does it matter?

Chapter 7: The Tribulation: Going from Bad to Worse

1. Why do you think God wanted us to know about the horrible events which will occur during the tribulation?

2 Are there current events and circumstances which cause you to think that the time of the tribulation is approaching? What about technological advances? Name a few of them and describe how they connect with the events that the Bible describes happening during the tribulation.

3. Do you think it is possible for a person to have such a dynamic personality that he can convince the majority of the world to follow his leadership? Describe how the world may react to the rise of the Antichrist.

4. During the end of the tribulation, life will be horrible for those people who refuse to give their allegiance to the Antichrist. Make a list of the emotions and fears that these people will have as they endure persecution and try to survive in a world dominated by the Antichrist.

Chapter 8: The Second Coming: Here Comes the King

1. How can your knowledge of the second coming as a future event give you confidence as you live your life now?

2. Does it bother you that Jesus is returning to uttterly crush His enemies?

3. In what ways does the biblical concept of the coming millennium differ from the world's concept of the "New Millennium"? In what ways are they the same?

Chapter 9: Judgment Day: Here Comes the Judge

1. Why do people fear death?

2. Imagine that you are guilty of committing a capital crime for which the mandatory sentence is the death penalty. The day for your sentencing has arrived. There are no more opportunities for an appeal. The judge enters the courtroom. You are instructed to stand before the judge to receive the pronouncement of your sentence. What are your feelings?

3. Use the scenario from the previous question, except this time, just as the judge is to make his pronouncement of your death sentence, the phone rings. It is the governor, and she is calling to grant you a pardon. Now, what are your feelings?

Chapter 10: Heaven: Our Greatest Hope

1. Describe a time when you thought about heaven as a kid. Are any of these images still real to you now?

2. Why do you think the Bible isn't more specific when it comes to heaven?

3. Who are the first three people you want to meet and talk to in heaven?

4. What's the difference—if any—between "endless time" and "timeless-ness"?

Chapter 11: Act Now! Limited Time Offer

1. People have a lot of misconceptions about what it means to be a Christian. What are some of these wrong impressions? What does it really mean to be a Christian?

2. Review the descriptions about Hell on pages 257-260. With the prospect of such horror, why do people refuse to accept God's offer to save them from it?

3. Imagine that you hear a knock on the front door of your home. When you open the door, you see Jesus Christ standing there. He says that He wants to have a meal with you in your home. Are you prepared to invite Him in? What will you talk about? What are you dying to ask Him? What will He ask you about yourself?

4. There are six categories of people described on pages 301-305. Each category has a different response to Christ. Which category best describes you? Are you content to stay in that category? If not, what is the hang up?

Chapter 12: Don't Wait Until You Are Dead to Get a Life

1. As you live your life now, in what ways do you feel the tension between your permanent future home and your temporary earthly one?

2. What is your greatest fear? How can you overcome that fear now?

3. Why do you think people in some parts of the world have it so good, while others are suffering because of their faith?

4. What can you do to let God "under your skin" now as you look forward to being with Him in the future?

Index

We've included this Index to help you find a particular topic, person or place. It doesn't include everything . . . just the stuff we thought you would be most interested in. If you can't find what you're looking for here, try scanning the Table of Contents or the "What's Ahead" section at the beginning of each chapter.

Also in the
Bruce & Stan's Guide Series:

BRUCE & STAN'S GUIDE TO GOD

by *Bruce Bickel and Stan Jantz*

Where did God come from? How do I know what I believe is true? Questions about the basics of the faith need straightforward answers. And here they are . . . in this fresh, user-friendly guide to the Christian life designed to help new believers get started or recharge the batteries of believers of any age. With humorous subtitles, memorable icons, and learning aids, the authors present even difficult concepts in a simple way. Perfect for personal use or group study.

BRUCE & STAN'S GUIDE TO THE BIBLE

by *Bruce Bickel and Stan Jantz*

First came *Bruce & Stan's Guide to God,* a fresh, new approach to making Christianity easy to understand—even the hard parts! Now Bruce and Stan use the same popular format to inspire readers to make sense of and *enjoy* the Bible. Encouraging readers to move immediately into interesting and productive Bible study, Bruce and Stan continue their clear, practical style of communicating information—with plenty of humor sprinkled throughout.